San Agustín

Art and Civilization of Indian America
General Editor Dr. Michael Coe

Gerardo Reichel-Dolmatoff

San Agustín

A Culture of Colombia

Praeger Publishers
New York · Washington

Books that matter

Published in the United States of America in 1972
by Praeger Publishers Inc.,
111 Fourth Avenue, New York, N.Y. 10003
All rights reserved
Library of Congress Catalog Card Number: 70–143979
Printed in Great Britain

Contents

This book owes its existence to the initiative of a friend and colleague of many years, Dr. Michael D. Coe, of Yale University, who suggested I write it for a new series under his editorship.

Many books, some of them splendid works with an abundance of fine illustrations, have been published in recent years on the subject of Pre-Columbian art and archaeology, but it is evident that most of them have concentrated on the great achievements in the main centers of American aboriginal civilizations, Mexico-Guatemala and Peru. Although these publications have made a vast contribution in bringing the artistic developments and mores of these ancient peoples to a wider circle of interested readers, it is also true that they have often overshadowed the accomplishments of many less well-known aboriginal cultures, which nevertheless are important expressions of artistic creativity. San Agustín is a case in point; hidden away in a remote mountain valley of the Colombian Andes, the stone monuments of its long-forgotten people are still very little known beyond the narrow circle of specialists whose researches, published in professional journals or out-of-print books, are too often inaccessible to the common reader. But there can be no doubt that local cultures such as San Agustín have much to offer to the general reading public, and that was why I gladly agreed to write this book.

In gathering the materials, I relied partly on my own excavations in the San Agustín region and partly on the research carried out by many distinguished colleagues. Among them, the eminent figure of Konrad Theodor Preuss deserves a prominent place, and next to him I must mention the Spanish scholar José Pérez de Barradas and Luis Duque Gómez, the Colombian archaeologist. All three have dedicated much effort to the study of this prehistoric culture.

My own field research in San Agustín was sponsored by the Instituto Colombiano de Antropología of the Ministry of Education and by the Universidad de los Andes at Bogotá. My sincere gratitude is due to both these institutions.

I am deeply grateful as well to the University of Cambridge (especially Corpus Christi College), which, by honoring me with a visiting scholarship, offered an ideal environment for compiling my manuscript and provided me with its unexcelled library facilities.

I also wish to express my gratitude to Alec Bright, from whose careful revision my manuscript has benefited greatly, and to Pauline Bright, whose patience and artistry produced the line drawings that illustrate the text. Many thanks are due, finally, to my friends in San Agustín, who accompanied me often over the mountain trails of their valley, and who did much to introduce me to the lore and lay of the land.

Cambridge-Bogotá,
December, 1970

Fig. 1   Principal topographical features of Colombia.

Chapter One

The Hidden Valley

Few countries in Latin America—indeed, in the whole world—present more complex geographical features than Colombia, which occupies the northwestern corner of the great South American triangle. Set amid the semiarid Caribbean lowlands, the grassy Orinoco plains, the Amazon rain forests, and the damp jungles of the Pacific seaboard, the interior of the country is divided by huge mountain ranges that traverse its entire length and separate it into innumerable valleys and plains, giving it an extremely varied topography and a wide range of climatic conditions.[1]

To the south—from Chile to Ecuador, and passing through Bolivia and Peru—the Andes form a cohesive chain of mountains, which branch off here and there, only to merge again into massifs and towering peaks from which radiate new cordilleras and valleys. But, north of the equator, on entering Colombia, the Andean system loses its relatively simple structure and begins to diverge sharply in different directions, its whole design changing and expanding into a new pattern. Here, in the southern provinces of Colombia, approximately between the towns of Pasto and Popayán, a vast mountainous knot arises, the so-called Colombian Massif, and from this point three main ranges begin to separate, forming what has come to be designated the Northern Andes, composed of the Eastern, Central, and Western cordilleras. At this central massif the Colombian landscape begins to unfold like a splendid multicolored fan, spreading out its mountains and valleys from the evergreen tropics to the bleak and cold highlands, from arid, wind-blown deserts to the lush temperate slopes of the subtropical zone.

The main structural feature of the country comprises these three mountain ranges, which in turn divide Colombia into three major units: the Andean region, the coastal lowlands, and the eastern lowlands. When speaking here of the Andes, we must keep in mind that Colombia is not an "Andean" country in the same sense as Peru, Ecuador, or Bolivia, for we do not find in it the vast expanses of barren highlands or the enormous snow-covered mountain chains we tend to associate with an Andean landscape. Colombia is a lush and green country in comparison with the Central Andes, and its mountain systems are considerably lower to the north of the equator. It is important to realize that the two coastal lowlands, the Pacific and the Caribbean, have very different geographical characteristics, the former being jungle country with a fringe of mangrove swamps and a very high rainfall, and the latter mostly

1 Upper Magdalena Valley northeast of San Agustín.

dry and covered with shrubs. The eastern lowlands are also subdivided into two quite different areas: the savanna-covered Orinoco plains and the rain forests of the Northwest Amazon.

But each area outlined above is subdivided into innumerable smaller units and microenvironments in which climate, relief, soil conditions, slope exposure, rainfall distribution, wind circulation, and plant cover are combined in the most varied ways. There are more than twenty arid or semiarid regions in Colombia, and some twenty others are covered by *ciénagas* (swamplands). There are also glaciers and deserts, narrow V-shaped valleys and broad alluvial plains, cold highland basins, and dense cloud forests. The major seasonal variations in climate are marked

not by changes in temperature but by variations in humidity and rainfall. In the inter-Andean valleys this diversity reaches its highest complexity and forms an intricate pattern of small interlocking microclimates. This extreme physical diversity of the Colombian landscape is, of course, linked in many ways to a marked cultural regionalism that has persisted from prehistoric times to the present—an important consideration for the archaeologist studying the ways in which environmental factors are related to cultural activities.

The cordilleras are the backbone of Colombia. Upon entering the country from the south, the wide sweep of the Andes breaks up into three ranges divided by the two great inter-Andean river valleys: the

2 View of Magdalena ravine from Chaquira site.

Magdalena and the Cauca, both of which traverse the country in a general south-to-north direction. The Magdalena River, Colombia's largest, runs for some 1,550 kilometers (969 miles) between the eastern and central ranges, and the Cauca River runs parallel to it, between the central and western ranges. The sources of these two large rivers lie close together in the Colombian Massif, and just as close to them lie the headwaters of other large rivers, which, however, flow in quite different directions; the Patía River flows westward toward the Pacific Coast, while the Caquetá and Putumayo rivers, both almost as long as the Magdalena, flow to the southeast and form part of the immense river system of the Northwest Amazon basin. The Colombian Massif is thus a pivotal point from which many of the most important rivers flow in different directions, accompanied by mountain ranges that radiate from it like an enormous fan.

Today the Massif is a wild, solitary mountain country, remote and inhospitable, sparsely inhabited by Indian peasants and some mestizo settlers. But it was not so in ancient times. Long before the arrival of the Spaniards, generations of aboriginal peoples had occupied these mountain-folds, establishing in them some of the strangest and most impressive monuments known to American prehistory. Near the headwaters of the Magdalena River there arose, over centuries and millennia, a large center of aboriginal life, whose peoples made these isolated valleys their home and whose mute remains still dominate the hilltops of these remote mountains.[2]

San Agustín—the name of a small Spanish settlement founded some-time in the early seventeenth century—has become synonymous with an extensive archaeological area that only in recent years has begun to attract the world's attention to one of the most important centers of aboriginal American stone sculpture. Hidden away in the mountainfolds, accessible only by tortuous roads or mule trails, its prehistoric monu-ments dot a large area of gentle slopes that descend from the eastern flanks of the Massif. The main valley, crossed by many small affluents of the upper Magdalena River, is surrounded by dark, forest-clad moun-tain chains, interrupted here and there by isolated peaks, but open toward the northeast where the Magdalena widens and begins to divide the Central and Eastern cordilleras in its course northward. The entire region is characterized by low, rolling hills that form chains and clusters, extend-ing over hundreds of square kilometers. Occasionally, higher elevations alternate with small peaks, while at other spots there are groups of low dome-shaped hills of approximately equal height.

When one ascends the upper Magdalena Valley the oppressive heat of its dry tropical climate soon gives way to a pleasantly temperate air, and as one approaches San Agustín the climate becomes increasingly cool until it reaches a median temperature of some 18°C. (48°F.). At noon, under the brilliant mountain sun, it may be hot, but, in the late afternoon, when the sun is setting behind the high ranges in the west, the air becomes chilly. Abrupt temperature changes are quite frequent. From the tropical lowlands hot air currents ascend and, reaching the San Agustín valley,[3] meet the cold winds proceeding from the Andean south, with the result

13

that rainfall is abundant but intermittent. Sudden showers and dazzling sunshine alternate, and at night the temperature drops sharply when the cold Andean wind enters the valley.

Fertile, well-irrigated soils, the yearly rainfall distribution, and the absence of flooding and erosion make this valley a favorable spot for agricultural purposes. At a mean altitude of 1,800 meters (5,905 feet) above sea level, the highly productive earth bears a wide variety of indigenous American plants, such as maize, sweet manioc, white carrot, sweet potatoes, cucurbits, beans, groundnuts, pineapples, and many fruit-bearing trees (peachpalm, avocado, and guava trees are abundant). Two maize harvests a year are the rule, and the vegetative cycle of many root crops is only about seven months.

Not only has the hill country around San Agustín a high agricultural potential, but it shares the natural and agricultural resources of the neighboring highlands and the hot lowlands, both within one or two days' walking distance. On market day, when the Indian peasants flock to the village from their remote fields and homesteads, the different food complexes—Andean, temperate, and tropical—meet at San Agustín and bear witness to the variety and abundance of natural resources.

This phenomenon—that of a relatively flat, highly productive valley occupying an intermediate position between fertile highlands and lowlands, both lying at a close distance—is not at all common in Colombia. On the contrary, the temperate slopes of the Northern Andes are more often steep and eroded, forming a very broken terrain, and the cold uplands or the tropical plains are far away and of difficult access. Not so at San Agustín, however: there, a wide, temperate basin of low hills is connected by gentle slopes to the cold highlands and the tropical lowlands, occupying a privileged position in the Colombian Andes.

No wonder, then, that this region has always attracted many peoples, some from quite distant parts, who settled in these hills until they themselves were uprooted or absorbed by the arrival of newcomers who, in their turn, were looking for a congenial place to settle. Indeed, archaeological records show that the valley of San Agustín was occupied in the past by several different groups of aboriginal peoples who were drawn there by the promise of its fertile soils.

Another natural advantage the region enjoys is the ease of communication by overland trails with many different and more distant geographical districts. Quite close to the valley of San Agustín is the lowest depression in the entire cordillera, leading down to the Northwest Amazon. Near the old Indian village of Mocoa, in the eastern foothills of the mountains, the headwaters of the Caquetá and Putumayo rivers, which flow into the immense rain forests of the Amazon basin, lie close together, and to the northeast another mountain pass, located at the foot of the Sumapaz massif, leads to the headwaters of the Guaviare, a large river that empties into the Orinoco. Other mountain passes, all of them of easy access, form natural communication routes with the Cauca Valley and, from there and the Patía River, to the Pacific Coast. Toward the south and the Ecuadorian highlands there are other mountain passes. If we add to this the opening toward the north and the Magdalena Valley, we can see that the San Agustín area, although hidden in the Andean core-land, nevertheless lies at the crossroads of several major natural migration and trade routes. Over these mountain passes peoples and ideas have moved back and forth for centuries, their coming and going helping to shape local cultural developments, be it by trade, migration, or invasion. The San Agustín valley was thus a link, an articulation point where different cultural traditions met and fused, and from which new impulses eventually spread to other regions.

The dark, abysmal ravine of the Magdalena River cuts straight across this green, undulating hill country. Abruptly, at the foot of the gently rolling hills, its sheer rocky walls appear, dropping suddenly into the dark dampness of the thundering river that cuts through the rocks, winding rapidly eastward to its outlet toward the open valley. From high above, on both sides, tumbling cascades cover the black boulders with their spray and foam, disappearing into the deep-cut gorge.

When standing on the rolling plateau and looking out over the land toward the fringe of mountains on the horizon, one would hardly suspect the existence of this deeply eroded ravine that divides the landscape into two sections. One suddenly observes this cleft only when approaching the breathtaking precipice where, hundreds of feet below, the Magdalena River breaks through the stony walls and cliffs of the narrow gorge before flowing out onto the open sunlit plain. Today the river marks the boundary between two municipalities, San Agustín on the right bank and San José de Isnos on the left. But no doubt it has always formed a dividing line between two regions, a division that presumably was of importance in prehistoric times.

Another major topographical feature is noteworthy: The outlines of the chains and clusters of elevations that form the horizon on every side are all quite similar. Indeed, for the visitor who is being told their local names, it is often difficult to distinguish between them, because their shapes are so uniform. But one hilltop stands out, the Cerro de la Horqueta, or "Forked Hill." This ancient volcano, whose exploded top gives it an M-shaped outline, occupies a prominent position. Located close to the Magdalena ravine, its characteristic silhouette can be seen from far off and from whatever other elevation on which the beholder may be standing. Although only slightly higher than the surrounding hills, this striking formation dominates the landscape, and again one wonders what its strange shape and central position meant to the ancient inhabitants.

There is no lack of water around San Agustín. The main river, as I have pointed out, is of difficult access, breaking its course through canyons and gorges, but between the hill ranges and all around them are many small streams, rivulets, and springs providing abundant water. Such major affluents as the Sombrerillos or the Matanzas River have cut fairly deep valleys, but none of them as impressive as the Magdalena ravine.

There is more to a landscape than what is implied by the term ecology. Archaeology is—or should be—the study of prehistoric man in nature, the study of cultures evolving in a certain physical setting that gave meaning and perspective to life and that, far from being a mere scenic backdrop, was an essential part of the historical processes the study is trying to reconstruct. The archaeologist should, therefore, look at the landscape not only in terms of its natural resources, economic potential, trade routes, and communications, but also as the setting in which man established his moral order and his social code. The seasonal harvest of wild-growing fruits, the wanderings of the game animals, the waning of the moon, the movements of the stars, the colors, textures, shapes, and sounds of nature—all these things formed part of man's experience in the world, part of that essential *intelligence du milieu* that made a land both a habitat and a home, beyond considerations of food and shelter.

Again one is impelled to look over the rolling hills of the hidden valley and scan the horizon for meaning. What did this land mean to its ancient inhabitants? What were the origins of the cruel gods who ruled them and whose stony faces still stare out over the mountains, like so many guardians of a shrine?

3   Mesita A, West Barrow. Main statue in underground chamber.

4   Mesita A, East Barrow. Detail of Plate 16.

The country is difficult to travel through, on account of the numerous rivers and swamps . . . where many men die owing to the great labor they have to endure . . . for every day we are exposed to death in a thousand forms. . . . I have thought of nothing, by day and by night, but how to support myself and the handful of men God has placed under my charge.

These words, written by Vasco Núñez de Balboa in his letter to King Ferdinand II (March, 1513), wherein he reports on his explorations of northwestern Colombia, express the thoughts and fears of thousands of men who had come to the conquest of the New Kingdom of Granada— that immense, rugged country lying between the "barbarous Caribbee Shoare" and the realm of the Inca. Some years later (1541), Pedro Cieza de León, a simple soldier, wrote a sober account of the exploration and conquest of the Colombian interior provinces, not far from San Agustín:

I may truly affirm that in all my life I never suffered such hunger as during that journey, although I have served in some expeditions of discovery in which we underwent great hardships. We found ourselves in so sad a plight in these dense forests, where the sun could never penetrate, without roads, or guides, or any one to tell us whether we were far or near any inhabited part, that we were inclined to return.

But return they did not. "By the help of God, and with the aid of our own arms, with which we forced our way, we got through these forests." Cieza de León lived to write his extraordinary chronicle on the conquest of the great Indian chiefdoms of the Cauca Valley.[1]

When the Spanish conquistadors first entered the mountain fastnesses of the Colombian Massif early in the sixteenth century, they found themselves confronted by fierce Indian tribes whose guerrilla tactics harassed the invading troops wherever they went. Fighting their way across the territories of one warlike group after another, the Spaniards explored the headwaters of the Cauca and Magdalena rivers step by step, searching for an easy communication between the two great inter-Andean valleys. This was a most important route, because safe communication between Santa Fé de Bogotá and Quito, passing through Popayán, was a vital matter, and no efforts were spared to subdue the rebellious natives by whatever means could be found. In few countries of the New World

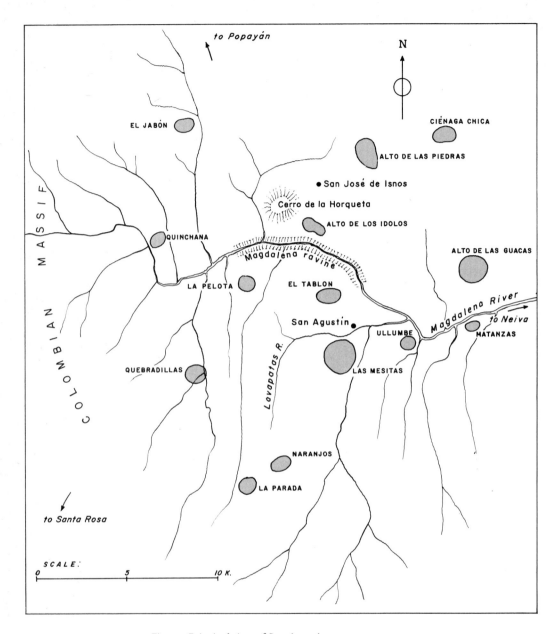

Fig. 2   Principal sites of San Agustín area.

was the Spanish conquest as savage and cruel as in Colombia, the land of El Dorado, the "Gilded Man," whose legend had fired the imagination of the first conquerors. Their greed for gold was matched only by the cunning and endurance of the Indians, whose minute knowledge of the terrain gave them an advantage over the slow-moving, hungry Spanish soldiers.

The chronicles tell of battles and ambushes, of noble deeds and treachery, of jungle diplomacy, and, finally, of the retreat of the natives and their submission to the Spanish overlords. The names of many tribes are mentioned but little else is recorded about them, their way of life, or their language, at least as far as the Indians of the Massif are concerned. The ancient records of 1628 that enumerate the tribes of the Magdalena headwaters speak of the Chumepa, Cambi, Yacua, Otongo, and others; some of the names—Guachico, Quinchana, or Maito—are still well-known place names and may be those of Indian groups that at that time lived in the surroundings of San Agustín.

The name San Agustín, however, is mentioned several years earlier in certain documents, from which it appears that during the entire seventeenth century the region was occupied by Indians who, after their first contact with the Spaniards, lived on rather friendly terms with them. Yet the same valley had been invaded a few generations before by a war-like tribe, the Andakí, who proceeded from the eastern slopes of the Cordillera and the Amazon forests. Bitter enemies of the peaceful San Agustín Indians, the Andakí, with the help of a missionary, left their homes in 1700 and went to live near Timaná under the protection of the Spaniards.[2] Only in 1753 was the deserted village site resettled, this time by a group of Quechua-speaking missionized Indians from Almaguer whom the Spanish authorities hoped would help in civilizing the few marauding groups of Andakí. Those were difficult times, and San Agustín was then hardly more than a small cluster of huts surrounded by a deep forest that had overgrown the fields and homesteads abandoned a half-century earlier.[3]

The local archives contain many records that speak of the settlement of the land surrounding the village, of the fertile soils and valuable minerals to be found, of building roads and a chapel, and of other administrative details. Strangely enough, however, no mention is ever made in the early chronicles of the huge stone monuments of the San Agustín valley. What had happened to them? Were they buried, hidden out of sight in the forest? Or did the Spaniards simply ignore them, there being more important matters to worry about? Or shall we one day find, perhaps, a bundle of yellow sheets containing the first eyewitness account of this site, somewhere in a Spanish archive or in the library of an ancient convent in Colombia? We do not know. All we can say is that, in the available sources dealing with the conquest and colonization of this part of the country during the sixteenth and seventeenth centuries, no reference can be found to this great center of prehistoric stone sculpture. Another half-century elapsed before the first record of its discovery appeared, and even this strange account was lost for two hundred years, coming to light only quite recently. The story of San Agustín follows.

In 1758 a lone Franciscan priest, Friar Juan de Santa Gertrudis, whose small mission center among the Indians of the Northwest Amazon was facing many difficulties, decided to cross the Eastern Cordillera and to travel to Santa Fé de Bogotá in order to appeal to the Spanish viceroy for help.[4] Accompanied by a few missionized Andakí Indians, Friar Juan ascended the eastern flanks of the Andes and, after many adventures, reached the headwaters of the Magdalena River at San Agustín, then a village of no more than five miserable huts. There were few people to

5　Drawing of tomb from Mesitas site, according to Rivero and Tschudi, 1825.

welcome the traveler, but among them there happened to be another cleric—a member of the Third Order from the bishopric of Popayán—the important colonial center in the Cauca Valley—who had established himself at San Agustín on a special mission and who now cheerfully offered his hospitality to the tired priest. Over a hearty evening meal the cleric confided to Friar Juan that he was an inveterate treasure hunter and that, with the help of some Indian laborers he had brought with him, he now was digging for buried gold among the ruins and monuments he had found scattered in the vicinity of the village. The cleric spoke at length about the strange monuments all around San Agustín and of the many burial sites there. He and his men had already dug nineteen tombs, but apart from potsherds and figurines they had found only a small golden earring.

Friar Juan listened in amazement; the next morning, while his Indians were still asleep after a night of merrymaking, he set out to see for himself and soon was standing in awe before a strange assembly of huge statues hewn out of solid rock. The site is described in his own words:

6 Drawing of two statues from Mesitas site, according to Rivero and Tschudi, 1825 (see Plates 41 and 52).

There are three bishops ... all of stone ... with their miters, and around the miters a wrought galloon, and in the middle a setting into which there must have been set some precious stone such as emeralds or amethysts.[5] They are dressed in their rochets which are fringed with lace, well-worked and beautiful. Only one has arms, but one can see that the left held a bishop's crozier while with the right he was giving his blessing. . . . Some fifteen paces off there are two more. . . . From there we went to see another monument. They are five Franciscan friars of the Observant Order shown from the knees up, carved of the same stone as the bishops. Two stand with hands folded and hidden in the sleeves ... two others are shown as if preaching. . . . The fifth wears a hood over his head and the hair in front is so finely worked that it looks quite real.

Friar Juan was greatly worried by this sight. To him there could be no doubt that these statues represented mitered bishops in pontifical garb and Franciscan friars, some of them shown as if exhorting a flock

23

of believers while others seemed to be standing in meditation, with arms crossed and hands hidden in the wide sleeves of their clerical robes. But, Friar Juan reasoned, since these images must surely be much older than the Order of Saint Francis, only the devil himself could have fashioned these strange images, perhaps to foretell the coming of Christ's ministers to the American infidels:

> I am convinced that the Devil made these statues, and I base my opinion on the fact that the natives of the Indies had no iron and, therefore, did not have tools to carve these images. However, from their oracles and idols they knew that the Sons of the Sun, that is, of the East, were about to arrive and were to conquer this land; and this is why I believe that the Devil made these statues and said to the Indians: Men like these, dressed in this manner, shall rule over this land.

The first description of the now famous archaeological site remained unpublished for nearly two centuries. It was discovered only recently in the public library of Palma de Mallorca, Friar Juan's native town, where he had died in 1799 after many years of travel and missionary work in the Kingdom of New Granada (present-day Colombia).

After Friar Juan came others, and with them the discovery that the stone images ranged through many types besides those the naïve missionary had written about. In 1797 Francisco José de Caldas (Colombia's scientist-martyr from the days of the Wars of Independence) visited San Agustín, and in his later writings he called public attention to the prehistoric monuments he found in the surroundings. Caldas, a typical eighteenth-century savant, wrote:

> San Agustín is inhabited by a few Indian families, and in its surroundings one finds traces of an artistic and industrious nation that has ceased to exist. Statues, columns, temples, altars, and an outsized image of the Sun show us the character and strength of a great people who lived on the headwaters of the Magdalena River. In 1797 I visited these sites, and with admiration I saw the works of art of this sedentary nation of which our historians have not transmitted to us the slightest notice. It would be very interesting to record and describe all the monuments which are found scattered in the vicinity of San Agustín. They might tell us to what point sculpture was developed among the inhabitants of these regions, and might teach us something about their religion and polity.[6]

Alexander von Humboldt, who traveled widely in Colombia in 1802 and whose voluminous writings did much to stimulate research in the natural sciences, never visited San Agustín, although he must have heard of it from his friend Caldas. At that time, during the first decades of the nineteenth century, the country was in turmoil. The long and bloody war of independence from Spanish rule was laying waste large regions of Colombia, and explorations ceased. Caldas, himself an ardent patriot for the Republican cause, was executed by the Spaniards, and with him the country lost its foremost scholar.

7   Statue from Mesita A. Watercolor by Manuel María Paz, Codazzi Expedition, 1853.

8 Guardian statue from Mesita A.
Watercolor by Manuel María Paz,
Codazzi Expedition, 1854
(see Plates 61 and 62).

A generation passed before another explorer visited San Agustín: in 1825 the Peruvian naturalist Mariano Eduardo de Rivero y Ustariz investigated the upper reaches of the Magdalena River and penetrated as far as Timaná and San Agustín. In 1851 he and the Austrian-born Johann Jakob von Tschudi published an account of their travels in the Andes, accompanied by a lavishly illustrated portfolio showing many Indian antiquities they had studied during their travels. Although their volume was devoted mostly to Peruvian prehistory, we find in it the first illustrations of San Agustín statues and a most interesting drawing of a ceremonial structure as it appeared then, along with a short text describing these monuments.[7] We find another report written shortly afterward, in 1853, by the Italian geographer General Agustín Codazzi who had traveled to the Massif on a mapping expedition for the Colombian Government. Codazzi wrote his lengthy report on the site and published an inventory of the statues, illustrated with a number of line drawings made after a series of watercolors by his traveling companion, the Colombian painter Manuel María Paz.[8]

In 1892 the Colombian general and naturalist Carlos Cuervo Márquez visited San Agustín on one of his many trips to the remoter regions of the country. A tireless explorer of Colombia's prehistoric past, Cuervo Márquez, not satisfied with a mere description of what he saw, became the first explorer to carry out small-scale excavations, the results of which led him to suggest a long time span of cultural development at San Agustín, together with certain relationships with the Central American and Andean civilizations. His widely read publications added substantially to the growing body of information on this culture, but it seems that the time was not yet ripe for a major expedition.[9] The Colombian civil wars, especially the last one (1899–1902), had thrown the country into misery and disorganization, and local scientific institutions could not be counted on under those circumstances.

Sporadic colonization of the San Agustín region by Indian and mestizo peasants had only begun late in the nineteenth century. The settlers lived in small, isolated homesteads; there were no large haciendas and no roads, except for the narrow mule trails. All occasional travelers or explorers who visited the region at the turn of the century spoke of the dense forest that covered the prehistoric monuments and of the tangled masses of vines, underbrush, and gigantic fallen trees under which lay half-buried statues and mounds. Torrential rainfalls eroded the trails, and the few bridges crossing the rivers were no more than slippery, swaying poles thrown across the current at convenient spots. Food resources were scarce, and the nearest town, Neiva, the district capital, more than a hundred miles away. To penetrate into the forest was an adventure only a few treasure-hunters or hardy naturalists cared to undertake. No wonder then that the hidden valley of San Agustín remained unexplored and shrouded in legend.

The account by Rivero and Tschudi and the later one by Codazzi had been widely read, and European scholars were becoming more and more interested in San Agustín. In 1911 the German geographer Karl Theodor Stöpel made a short visit to San Agustín to cast paper molds of some eighteen statues, but without carrying out any excavation.[10] Stöpel did, however, take many photographs, which gave a far more vivid impression than the amateurish drawings his predecessors had published with their reports. The next year, Stöpel presented an illustrated paper at the International Congress of Americanists in London.[11] It was Stöpel's enthusiastic appeal to his audience of archaeologists that, at long last, brought the first major scientific expedition to San Agustín.

In 1913 Konrad Theodor Preuss of the Museum für Völkerkunde in Berlin arrived in Colombia, where he was to spend several years laying the groundwork for a series of systematic studies in archaeology and ethnology. Even at that comparatively late date, reaching San Agustín was no easy matter. From Barranquilla, the Caribbean port at the mouth of the Magdalena River, it took Preuss twelve days by paddle steamer to reach Honda, a small town in the interior that marked the limit of steamship navigation. From there it was necessary to proceed on muleback, following the hot, arid, often barren valley of the river, which the Spanish conquistadors had named Valle de la Tristeza, or Valley of Sorrows. Five days later the small party arrived at Neiva, and it continued for three more days before the trail began to wind up the mountain slopes toward the temperate valleys of the Massif. "One feels lost here, as on a dead-end street," wrote Preuss. "Perhaps to this is due the oblivion in which the antiquities of this region have remained." At last they arrived at San Agustín, and, upon entering the village square, the tired archaeologist had his first glimpse of what was to be his task for the following months: fourteen huge statues were standing there in line, brought to the village by peasants and landowners, and Preuss, who had with him Codazzi's illustrated report, greeted the grim stony faces "as if they were old friends."

For the next three months Preuss traveled on horseback and foot over most of the valley and established a detailed catalogue of all the prehistoric monuments he was able to observe. At that time the land was still heavily wooded, with only a few trails leading from the village to some lonely homesteads, making the discovery of previously unknown stone carvings very tiresome and time-consuming work. These difficulties were increased by rainfall, disease, and lack of provisions. Besides photographs, exact measurements, and full descriptions of the monuments, Preuss took a large number of molds, which later permitted him to reconstruct the stone carvings for museum exhibits in Europe. Most of his researches were concerned with this tedious inventory. Excavations were limited to several mounds and burial sites, and no stratigraphic work was done, but Preuss clearly recognized that there was considerable time-depth to the cultural remains he was describing, that the statues dated from different periods. His scholarly and well-illustrated two-volume work (now long out of print) was published in 1929, and it remains the basic source on the archaeology of this region, especially in its descriptive aspects. This, then, was the first systematic survey of San Agustín sculpture, and the exhibits organized by Preuss, enhanced by fourteen original statues that he managed to take to Germany, introduced the European public to this strange aboriginal culture.[12]

Two Spanish-language editions of Preuss's work helped to awaken the interest of the local authorities, and in 1935 the Colombian Ministry of Education purchased a large tract of land near San Agustín in order to put the principal monuments under government protection, thus establishing the "Archaeological Park," as it is still called. Shortly afterward, in 1936–37, the first official Colombian excavations, patronized by the Ministry, were carried out under the direction of the Spanish archaeologist José Pérez de Barradas. This expedition, in which several Colombian archaeologists participated, notably Gregorio Hernández de Alba and Luis Alfonso Sánchez, discovered many new monuments, among others the famous bedrock carvings of the Lavapatas site. Details of tomb structure were investigated, together with the nature of several mounds, and a fairly large amount of pottery and lithic tools was collected.[13] In the years following, several smaller expeditions led by both Colombian and foreign scholars visited San Agustín and carried out sporadic explorations, but the principal work was accomplished by Luis Duque Gómez, for many years director of the Instituto Colombiano de Antropología, who not only excavated several major burial grounds but also took an active interest in the conservation of the site and of its major monuments. It is to these men that we owe most of what is known today about San Agustín's culture and its extraordinary stone carvings.

A certain trend is noticeable in all the books and articles written on San Agustín during the years when different expeditions worked at that site: a fascination with statues and tombs. More and more sculptures were discovered and described, and hundreds of tombs were opened, but because few other aspects were ever investigated, a rather one-sided impression soon began to emerge from the mass of published reports. The emphasis on stone carvings and burial practices was beginning to obscure all other aspects of the prehistoric scene. San Agustín was being described as a large ceremonial center, a huge necropolis hidden in the mountainfolds, a place of nothing but tombs and funerary monuments. It seemed that the task of archaeology had become that of pondering death instead of reconstructing life. Because of almost exclusive concentration on the more spectacular aspects of the site, the vital problems of typology and chronology were all too often overlooked, and little was accomplished to establish a time scale that would show successive phases of development and changing patterns of past life.

It is apparent now that a new type of research is due at San Agustín, a more integrated approach that might tell us more about its early beginnings, the spread of settlement patterns, and the economic bases of its ancient inhabitants. But this stage of scholarship is just beginning, and from its first tentative results one can deduce that there is still much to be discovered in these valleys that might contribute significantly to American archaeology.

9　Cerro de la Horqueta. Slopes are covered with cropmarks and outlines of ancient fields.

Chapter Three

Prehistoric Settlement

The first thing to do is look at the landscape as a whole. Our visual memory is sometimes overburdened, and perhaps deformed, by the many illustrations of architectural features and monuments we have looked at so often, by the images of statues and tombs, of pottery types and decorative motifs. We often lose sight of the wider context of the land within which these objects were created, and it becomes necessary to look at the landscape afresh, as if for the first time, because the land, too, is a cultural object that has been molded and transformed into what those ancient peoples called their home. Thousands of feet have trodden this soil; thousands of hands have touched it, opening trails, clearing fields, leveling house sites. Those long-forgotten hands moved stones, felled trees, and put a row of slabs across the riverbed or opened the outlet of a nearby spring. Here a stepping stone was set into the steep trail; over there a drainage ditch was dug or a natural depression in an outcropping boulder was used to polish some object, perhaps an ax.

The rolling hills of San Agustín, clad in brilliant shades of green and separated by innumerable valleys, do not form a single compact site. There are no large plains, no level terraces or valley bottoms where large permanent settlements might have developed, no centers from which a growing village might have spread over the nearby countryside. The very formation of the land, broken into a pattern of hillocks, of clusters of hills and ridges, forced people to separate and to circumscribe their settlements within small areas, often quite close together, but nevertheless limited and isolated from their neighbors. There is then no core, no center to speak of, but dozens of larger or smaller sites, or groups of settlements, that cover the hilltops and the mountainfolds to the horizon. Consequently, San Agustín is not a coherent archaeological site but, rather, a large cluster of many individual sites, each with its own physical characteristics and history. Some—perhaps many—were occupied in the same period, while others were abandoned. The ever changing flux of spread and concentration, of stability and change, made one region at times more prominent than others, more permanently occupied, or perhaps more easily surrendered or abandoned. The interplay of social organization, land use, the level of technology, war and peace, and trade and religion led to the emergence or decline of this or that settlement over the centuries.

We must then take a closer look at these hills and gentle slopes around San Agustín. Much of the land has been cleared only in recent times.

Even in the 1920's and 1930's heavy forest still covered much of the countryside. Only during the late 1930's and early 1940's did the homesteaders begin to open up the land for their cattle and maize fields. This process continues now, and on the horizon there still are vast expanses of dark forest.

During much of the day the green hills, now covered with pastures and fields, follow one another in monotonous waves. But in the late afternoon, under the oblique rays of the declining sun, a play of shadows begins and suddenly another landscape takes shape: straight lines begin to cross the fields; faint shadows begin to outline plots and patches on the grassy slopes; here and there appear straight ridges, trails, boundaries, sudden changes in the color and type of plant cover. The ancient landscape is coming to life, transformed by man and shaped to his needs in prehistoric times.[1]

Other aspects of the landscape are striking. Somehow the contours of certain hills upon which stand statues or mounds are not quite natural; there are breaks in the gradients, and level places that seem too level to be natural. Soon it becomes clear that a large number of important earthworks and engineering features exist. Some of them were probably related in part to the transportation and construction of the monuments, but others were related to habitation sites. The labor force by which the stone monuments were manufactured and moved to their final destinations is another point of interest. Most of the statues or huge slabs that were used in construction are standing on hilltops or slopes, and quite often the rock formations from which they were carved are a considerable distance away, in the valley bottoms. It is obvious that these objects, weighing many tons, could not have been carried on poles but had to be pushed and dragged at ground level, perhaps on wooden rollers. No matter how many people were gathered to perform this task, it is reasonable to suppose that they built some sort of ramps or earthen banks. As a matter of fact, by following the contours of the hills and observing how the individual elevations and ranges are linked or separated, it is possible to trace some of these routes of access and to locate sections of the ramps and stretches where the ground has been leveled or where a connecting ridge has been built between two elevations to facilitate the transportation of the stones.

While one watches out for possible traces of an ancient network of heavy transport routes, it also becomes evident that other aspects of the landscape were transformed in prehistoric times. There are flat expanses that, as excavation proved, had been filled in and leveled as habitation sites; there are ramparts and artificial ridges seemingly built to serve as defenses.

It is this transformation of the landscape that will introduce us to the prehistoric life of San Agustín, which we must view in terms of large earthworks and fields; of habitation sites and roads; of a people working, cultivating the soil, and shaping the land into a cultural surrounding.

10 Mesitas, South Barrow. Remains of subterranean chamber. ▷

One must visualize a process of adaptation to an environment, a process carried out in a highly propitious region—economically and strategically, in terms of outside contacts and local contiguity—that had attracted people for thousands of years and where they settled and lived.[2]

From these observations we can deduce that the San Agustín area was peopled for long periods by fairly large sedentary groups that transformed the environment by intensive farming, road-building, numerous settlements, and the construction of large earthworks. There exist, of course, ceremonial aspects at San Agustín, but their importance certainly does not overshadow all others.

We must now narrow down our observations to individual sites and features. So far, about forty of these sites are known, and usually they are designated by their traditional local names, which allude to some aspect of nature or perhaps to some accident of history. These sites are scattered over an area of at least 500 square kilometers (190 square miles), covering large tracts of the municipalities of San Agustín and San José de Isnos, on both sides of the Magdalena River.

Close to the village, about four kilometers (two and a half miles) to the west, lies Las Mesitas, a major site, which—being easily accessible—has long been a center of attraction and research. The low hills lying between two affluents of the Naranjos River form a flat expanse with only a few irregular, shallow depressions, and it is obvious that the surface has been leveled artificially, at some spots by cutting and scraping off the soil, at others by filling in, until a fairly large plateau began to take shape, more or less triangular in outline. The outstanding features of this little plain are several groups of low, dome-shaped barrows or earthen mounds, which undoubtedly served ceremonial purposes.

At Mesita A, as the first group is called, the barrows consist of circular accumulations of earth, about twenty-five meters (eighty feet) in diameter and some four meters (thirteen feet) high, although originally they may have been considerably higher. In their centers are underground chambers each of which consists of a single rectangular room built of huge vertically set slabs roofed with a number of large, flat capstones. Within each central chamber one or more large statues were found standing or lying, and everything seems to indicate that these chambers, incorporated into the mounds, were funerary monuments. (These constructions are described in greater detail in Chapter Four.)

In the immediate vicinity of the barrows at Mesita A have been found several freestanding statues that were probably connected with these ceremonial structures. Mesita B lies about 180 meters (200 yards) to the northwest and consists of three large barrows, two of which originally contained a square central chamber, but which at present are almost completely destroyed. A large number of some of the most extraordinary statues are found at this spot, together with several large trough-shaped sarcophagi more than two meters (six feet, seven inches) in length. It is indeed a pity that all the earth-covered tombs from this and several other sites should have been destroyed by treasure-hunters.[3]

Crossing the plain of Mesita B toward the southwest, we find another group of statues in the vicinity of a small barrow called Mesita C, and

11   Mesita B, Northwest Barrow. Large triangular face.

12 Inza. Gold mask of jaguar-monster.

from here we continue to descend into the valley of a small river where the site of Lavapatas is located. Here the entire surface of the large bedrock over which shallow water flows is covered with intricate carvings. There are several square pools that have been cut out of the rock and that are connected by a series of meandering channels, which distribute the water in such a way that it cascades into the basins. The rock surface is adorned with a maze of relief figures of snakes, lizards, monkeys, and human figures wearing high headdresses—all bathed by the clear mountain stream. Climbing up the opposite river bank and ascending the slope, we arrive at the Alto de Lavapatas, another center of large stone carvings, including isolated heads and a large flat slab carved in the shape of a crouching animal.

Were we to continue walking toward the southwest we would soon find other sites: Los Naranjos and La Parada and, turning toward the west, the site of Quebradillas. Everywhere huge stone carvings stand on the hilltops, and everywhere middens, potsherds, obsidian chips, and traces of earthworks cover the ground. To the west of San Agustín there are several major sites—Cerro de la Pelota, El Tablón, and Alto de la China—all of them marked by stone sculptures and surface indications of settlements or burial grounds. In this area, the site of La Chaquira is a most spectacular spot, close to the deep ravine of the Magdalena River and commanding a splendid view over the abysmal mountain gorge with its tumbling cascades. No freestanding statues are found at this site, but the surfaces of enormous boulders have been covered with relief carvings of human beings and animals.

Still farther to the west, in the foothills of the highland area of the Páramo de las Papas, is Quinchana, a site where a small mound was discovered, topped by an accumulation of stones; it proved to contain the statue of a crouching woman, enclosed in a small cistlike chamber of rough slabs. In the immediate neighborhood a large number of cist graves were found. Abundant potsherds and the artificial leveling of the ground indicate the former existence of a large village.

East of San Agustín, across the Sombrerillos River, the mountainfolds and hills are covered with more sites. At the Alto de Lavaderos and other spots there are freestanding statues, sarcophagi, and many traces of earthworks. Smaller sites, bearing the names of homesteads, are scattered over the entire area: El Batán, La Estrella, Las Moyas, Purutal, Ullumbe, Matanzas. It would be difficult indeed to find a hilltop or a small river terrace where there are no vestiges of former occupation, whether in the form of stone carvings, potsherds, obsidian chips, or the remains of earthworks connected with house sites or ancient fields.

But as yet we have spoken only of the southern section of the archaeological area; on the left bank of the Magdalena River the sites continue, now in the municipality of San José de Isnos. The most spectacular site discovered thus far in this region is the Alto de los Idolos, a large hill in the shape of a horseshoe with its open end facing south. On its western arm are six large stone cists built of enormous slabs, each containing a monolithic sarcophagus, and near them stands a barrow with a central chamber and a huge female statue. On the eastern arm are also several

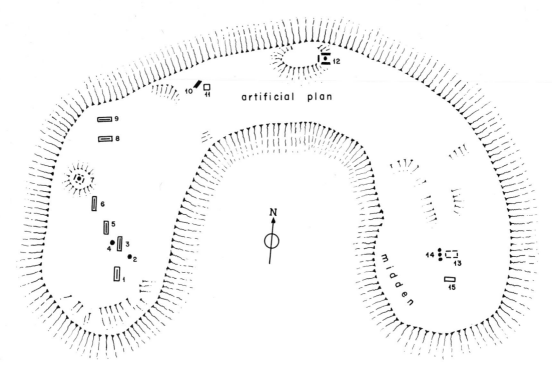

artificial plan

N

midden

1, sarcophagus; 2, perforated slab; 3, sarcophagus (Pl. 20); 4, statue (Pl. 45); 5, sarcophagus (Pl. 23); 6, sarcophagus; 7, barrow with chamber and statue (Pl. 58); 8, sarcophagus (Pl. 21); 9, sarcophagus (Pl. 22); 10, large inclined carved slab (Pl. 69); 11, shaft grave; 12, chambered barrow with statue (Pl. 43); 13, looted grave; 14, table-shaped "altar" (Pl. 99) and two small statues; 15, carved slab (Pl. 100).

Fig. 3   Sketch map of Alto de los Idolos.

burial mounds and some freestanding statues. The two branches of the horseshoe are connected by a large, slightly curved embankment consisting of an artificial fill several meters deep, on the northern edge of which stands another barrow; a slab-lined chamber can be seen on the periphery of the barrow. On the western end of the embankment is a deep shaft grave, and next to it an enormous inclined statue—perhaps more than four meters (thirteen feet) tall—has been sunk in the ground.

It would be a mistake to think that this extensive site served mainly ceremonial purposes and was only a burial place. In reality it was a large habitation site in which the ceremonial features are only secondary to other cultural remains. In fact, the whole upper part of the eastern section is a single stratified midden, a thick mantle many meters deep of occupational débris formed by generations of people who threw their refuse down the slopes, occasionally leveling the top to make space for more dwellings, while building up layer after layer of potsherds. At a certain point on the slope, the overflow stopped and the midden blended into the gradient of the hill, which—once covered with vegetation—looked like a natural formation. This, as we shall see later on, proves to be true of other hills as well. Excavations have shown that large sections of them are formed by dense and deep accumulations of occupational refuse, potsherds and stone tools, proving beyond doubt that these hills were essentially habitation sites. Excavations on several level sites, some of them quite broad, have shown that these too were once habitation areas. In some spots the density of the refuse is truly extraordinary. For example, a single stratum some twenty centimeters (eight inches) thick in a four-square-meter (4.8-square-yard) pit, contained more than 15,000 potsherds. Many of the flat areas on which statues or barrows stand were habitation zones, artificially leveled and densely peopled for long periods of time, judging by the enormous amount of refuse discarded and thrown down the slopes or into nearby gullies.

But let us return to the Alto de los Idolos. Quite close, toward the northwest, rises the broken cone of the Cerro de la Horqueta, the Forked Hill, previously mentioned. Its flanks are covered with faint lines that mark ancient fields and trails, and all around its base indications of human settlement abound—small embankments for house sites, drainage ditches, and potsherds, eroded on the surface or washed out of the walls of gullies. From the Alto de los Idolos we can scan the horizon and point out many other major sites: the Alto de las Piedras, a few kilometers to the north, with some of the most interesting stone carvings; the Alto de las Guacas; the hills around Ciénaga Chica; the sites of Obando, El Jabón, Granada, Mondeyal, Salado Blanco and many more. In the distance the chains of hills continue, some covered with green pastures and fields, others still heavily wooded. When the peasants flock to the village of San José de Isnos on a market day, there is no end to their tales of statues and tombs, of pots and stones, and of buried treasures to be found on their land. While tilling the soil, looking for timber, or hunting, they have all found some remains of the ancient inhabitants, and they can point out more sites than could ever be investigated by archaeologists.

13   Mesitas, South Barrow. Detail of construction.

Chapter Four

One of the most outstanding features of ancient San Agustín is its barrows. At Mesita A, these circular ceremonial structures measure about twenty-five meters (eighty-two feet) in diameter; their present height is about four meters (thirteen feet). Both barrows incorporate tombs formed of enclosures made of very large stone slabs, in the center of which stand one or more statues. The first of these mounds, called the East Barrow, originally contained a single rectangular sepulchral chamber in its center. The walls of the chamber were formed by large undressed slabs with irregular edges, set vertically in the ground, and it was roofed with several still larger capstones. The size of some of the slabs used in this construction is truly amazing, if one thinks in terms of the labor involved in putting them into place; one of them measures 4.4 meters (14.4 feet) in length, 3.06 meters (10.04 feet) in width, and 28 centimeters (11.02 inches) in thickness, while others are about three meters (ten feet) long and 1.50 meters (4.9 feet) wide. It is characteristic, both here and at other sites, that these slabs were not dressed to straight edges and faces; rather, they show only a few coarse retouchings. The chamber was high enough to stand in, and it seems that its floor was somewhat below ground level, having been dug into the original surface before the earth cover was put over the entire construction.

There has been much discussion among archaeologists concerning the true nature of these barrows, and some authors—notably Pérez de Barradas—believe that they were public places of worship. Accordingly, it has been said that one side of the chamber was left open and that from there a narrow stone-lined and stone-roofed passage led to the outside at the edge of the mound. In other words, the San Agustín barrows were described as very similar in plan to the megalithic passage graves of Western Europe. Yet there is very little evidence that would support this theory. It is true that the central chamber is "open" on one side, but this is the work of grave-robbers, and there is no evidence of a passage leading to the outside.[1]

All the chambered barrows discovered so far contain at least one large statue, and it seems that, in some, several statues were placed close together in the chamber or crypt. The East Barrow was described in 1853 by Codazzi, who published a reconstruction of it showing that the chamber contained two column-shaped additional statues that served as atlantes, sustaining the foremost capstone of the roof; he did not, however,

14 and 15   Mesita A, East Barrow. Main
statue and (right) detail of the head.

mention the central statue. Preuss found that the chamber had collapsed,
having been destroyed by treasure-hunters, and rediscovered the main
statue (Plate 14) lying on its back, with the two atlantes close by (Plate 16).
From the way the statues fell, Preuss deduced that the atlantes were
standing behind the main image, in the far corners of the chamber.

The response these images struck in ancient times in the beholder or,
rather, the believer must have been one of fearful awe. The main image
represents a monstrous being, half man and half beast, carved in the round
from a huge block of pale yellowish stone, and measures more than two
meters (six feet, seven inches) in height. The naked body is encircled by a
double, cordlike belt with a complicated knot over the right hip, and the
oversize head bears a ferocious face, huge pointed fangs protruding from
the gaping mouth, and enormous, blindly staring eyes. The two atlantes
are somewhat taller, measuring 2.55 meters (8.37 feet) in height, and
represent human beings—warriors or guardians perhaps—who in a
menacing gesture grasp huge clubs in their upheld hands. Each of their
heads is topped by a column-shaped carving that shows a strange beastly
face and part of a body, as if crouching or hanging over the back of the
statue. It is evident that these weird sculptures represent the guardians
or defenders of the sepulchral chamber, and their similarity in form and
gestures suggests that they once flanked the main statue. Codazzi mentions
that in 1853 there were two more statues in this chamber, one of which,
holding a "hammer and chisel" in its hands, was removed from the site
in 1869 and brought to the village square, from where it was transported
to Bogotá in 1907. At present it stands in the entrance hall of that city's
Museo del Oro. The other sculpture mentioned by Codazzi as pertaining

42

to this barrow is probably the large statue with crossed arms that can be found today in the so-called Bosque de las Estatuas, or Grove of Statues, in the Archaeological Park of San Agustín, where a large number of stone carvings from different sites have been set up for public display.

The West Barrow of Mesita A contains a similar crypt, although a somewhat smaller one. The central chamber is about two meters (six feet, seven inches) wide and corresponds in its structural details to that of the East Barrow. The statue that Codazzi found standing inside the chamber (but that by the time of Preuss's visit had been dragged out) represents another aspect of the monstrous personage with pointed fangs (Plate 17). They too are topped by columns, which are not carved in the shape of secondary figures. Codazzi says that behind the main statue stood a stone carving of "two monkeys," but this has disappeared.[2]

The two barrows of Mesita A are set close together, with only some twenty meters (sixty-six feet) separating them. Part of the function of the earth covering of these tombs was undoubtedly to hold together the entire structure, and at several barrows one can observe that around the periphery a circle of upright slabs had been set, a kind of retaining wall, to keep the accumulated soil from eroding. In most cases these walls have crumbled or have been destroyed by treasure-hunters, and the ensuing denudation has led to the progressive leveling of the barrow. The South Barrow of Mesita B, for example, has been almost completely obliterated

and offers the dolmen-like aspect of a surface structure (Plate 10).[3]

Preuss was the first to mention that the main statue of the East Barrow of Mesita A showed traces of black and red paint, and this observation has been confirmed by other archaeologists and at other sites. It seems not only that the principal statues were painted with red, black, and yellow pigments but that the walling and roofing stones of the chambers were also covered on the inside with geometrical designs in these colors. Graffiti are frequent on the flat surfaces of the slabs that form the walls of the chambers (Figure 5).

The above description can be applied in general to most other barrows in the San Agustín area. At Mesita B, one statue represents a woman holding an infant in her arms (Plate 18), while the two atlantes are monstrous beings with ribbed bodies, protuberant eyes and grinning, fanged mouths (Plate 29). There were at least four other statues associated with this barrow, all of which show similar feline features: one of them carrying a snake (Plate 65), another bearing a fish (Plate 42), a third wearing a cylindrical cap (Plate 41), and a fourth with a protruding tongue that ends in a head (Plate 78).

The Northwest Barrow of Mesita B contained a large sepulchral chamber that has been destroyed almost completely; enormous slabs and part of the retaining walls are found lying about on the slopes and at the foot of the mound, and only the main statue—another feline personage—

16 (far left)   Mesita A, East Barrow. One of pair of guardian statues.

17 (left)   Mesita A, West Barrow. One of pair of guardian statues.

18   Mesita B, South Barrow. Figure holding infant.

Fig. 4   Painted slabs from subterranean chamber of South Barrow, Mesita B (after Pérez de Barradas).

is still standing on its original spot, being far too heavy to move (Plate 59). There are two pairs of atlantes on this barrow, from which we can deduce that originally there were two chambers. But we do not know which of the many sculptures that stand nearby might have been the main image of the second chamber. It may have been the one carrying a crescent-shaped face in its hands, which formerly stood on this barrow before being moved to the village square and then to the Grove of Statues (Plate 52). In connection with this barrow, Rivero's and Tschudi's illustration from 1825 is of interest. The illustration (Plate 5), although idealized and romantic, is not (according to the description given by these authors) an imaginary reconstruction but a rendering of a burial chamber as it appeared at that time. Yet which chamber? Rivero and Tschudi illustrate two statues from the Ullumbe site (Plate 6), the relief-carved slab from El Batán (Figure 14), and several statues from the Northwest Barrow; in other words, they visited this particular spot. However, the central image they illustrate is not the one we have just mentioned—the feline personage with the trophy head—but seems to show the back of a quite different statue, covered with the sculptured representation of an animal skin. The concentric circles on the inside of the right wall seem to represent a painted design. The sarcophagus lying in front of the chamber may well be one of two similar pieces that, at present, lie at the foot of the Northwest Barrow.

Of the two barrows at the Alto de los Idolos, one—located on the eastern branch—again contains a large statue with feline features (Plate 58), but in the barrow standing on the embankment between the hills, a female statue was standing, showing a rather placid-faced woman holding a cup in one hand (Plate 43). It may be noted here that this chamber was built on the periphery of the barrow, not at its center.

Several barrows stood at the El Tablón site and at least one at El Jabón. There are certainly many more of these burial mounds in the San Agustín area, located in still unexplored regions and overgrown by vegetation. We can hopefully suppose that some of them will be discovered and excavated by archaeologists and not by treasure-hunters. It would be of special interest to ascertain the relationship of these chambered barrows to other statues or sculptured stones that might be found in the surroundings, and also to investigate the possibility that the chambers and their barrows were chronologically correlated with other types of burials. In fact, the stone carvings associated with the barrows represent different styles, and this seems to indicate that these places of burial were in use for long periods of time, during which certain formal and symbolic trends developed.

Burial practices at San Agustín were extremely varied, and their relationship to barrow structures, statues, and habitation sites is far from clear. Some of the barrows containing chambers have been used as

Fig. 5 Large slab with incised figures from South Barrow, Mesita B (after Pérez de Barradas).

19   Alto de los Idolos. Horizontal shadow in the center indicates the extension of a midden accumulation.

general burial grounds, and a number of shallow pit graves have been found in the earth covering of the barrows—although it is possible that these were dug at a later date and were originally not connected with the main tomb structure. That occasionally a mound area (that is, the circular extension around a chambered barrow) might have been used as a cemetery is possible, but these graves seem to have a connection with a later period and not that when the barrows were built.

A rather common type of grave at San Agustín is the cist grave, an elongated rectangular box formed of several slabs set vertically in the ground and generally overlaid with a number of covering slabs. Some of them may have had a relief-carved slab as cover. The cist graves hold a single burial, with the body in a supine position. A number of these graves were found on the Mesita A site, some quite close to barrows, and others were found scattered here and there, sometimes within settlement zones. An interesting case is the Quinchana site, where a large female statue was found enclosed in a cistlike structure that was subsequently completely covered with a large accumulation of unshaped stones. In the surroundings of this mound a large number of cist graves were discovered, some of them within the stone-covered area. This, then, was evidently a sepulchral monument in which the statue was buried together with the dead.[4] A similar situation was found at the Mesitas site, where the cist grave contained not only a skeleton with associated items but also a statue.

Shallow pit graves containing single or multiple flexed burials constitute another type found frequently at San Agustín. In several cases, these more or less conical pits are fairly large and contain a number of

48

skeletons. Some of the pit graves are covered with irregular slabs, and in others the corpse was placed upon a large slab and then covered with earth.

Shaft graves provided with a lateral vault have been found at many sites. The vertical shaft, circular in cross-section and up to five meters (sixteen feet) deep, was dug into the soil, and at the bottom a vaulted chamber was excavated laterally; it contained the corpse and the grave offerings. The entrance to this side chamber was often closed with a heavy slab so that the soil with which the shaft was filled would not enter the grave itself. At the Alto de los Idolos, a very large and deep shaft grave shows traces of yellow, black, and red paint on the walls of the lateral vault.[5]

An extraordinary grave type is the monolithic sarcophagus. More than thirty of these heavy stone coffins have been found at San Agustín, all of them looted long ago by grave-robbers. There are several kinds: most of them are rectangular, elongated boxes, but some are of trapezoidal shape with rounded corners. The entire block, usually two meters (six feet, seven inches) long, was carefully hollowed out, and in most cases the walls were polished to show no tool marks. Several sarcophagi are adorned with carved heads on the outside. One of the sarcophagi of the Alto de los Idolos is provided with a pair of handle-like extensions on each end (Plate 20) and, like several others, shows a deep groove or duct cut into the end of the wall. Speculation as to the function of this groove has produced the suggestion that it provided a passage for the soul; this may be so, but it is also quite possible that the groove had a more practical function as a hold for a lever to adjust or lift the heavy lid. The lids are very heavy slabs cut to the size of the coffin, and in several cases the surface is carved in relief with a reclining figure (Plate 23). Burials in monolithic sarcophagi are almost always enclosed in stone cists, similar

20   Alto de los Idolos. Monolithic sarcophagus surrounded by fallen slabs, which once formed a large cist grave.

21 Alto de los Idolos. Stone sarcophagus and remains of large cist grave.

to, but larger than, the common cist graves and formed of six or eight huge undressed slabs topped with capstones. The sarcophagi always occupy a prominent spot at all sites; at the Mesitas site they are close to the largest (northwestern) barrow, and at the Alto de los Idolos they are located at the highest point of the ridge and close to a chambered barrow.

Stöpel gives an interesting description of a major tomb found near Isnos, and, although he does not mention its exact site, it appears that he is referring to the Alto de los Idolos. By his account, a large barrow excavated there proved to contain a square chamber, the walls of which had been constructed of large rounded cobblestones, up to a height of two meters, the inside being roughcast with a kind of mortar. This chamber, which measured about two meters square, was roofed with several flat capstones, and the entire structure was covered with earth. Inside the chamber were three stone sarcophagi set side by side.

Occasionally, it seems, wooden coffins were used, also covered with stone slabs bearing relief carvings: on the Alto de Lavapatas, a large wooden trough, provided with two pairs of handles, was found covered with a heavy slab shaped like a crouching animal (Plate 101). No doubt these sarcophagi were destined only for the burial of certain people,

50

22 (above) Alto de los Idolos. Monolithic sarcophagus surrounded by upright slabs.

23 Alto de los Idolos. Relief–carved slab covers a sarcophagus enclosed in a cist.

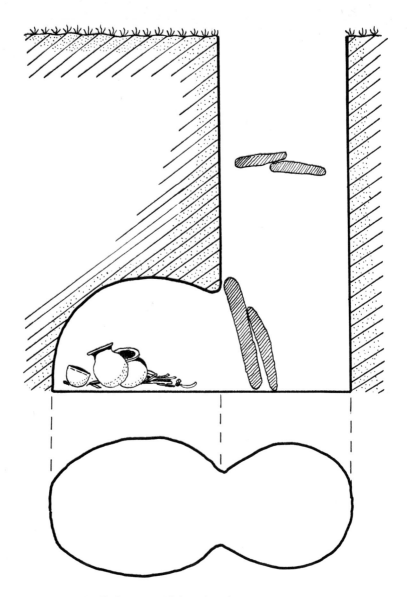

Fig. 6   Mesita A. Shaft grave with lateral vault.

perhaps chiefs, shamans, or warriors, and it is to be regretted that so far not a single one has been excavated by an archaeologist.

Urn burials have been reported from several tombs, mostly of the shaft-and-chamber type. Large pottery vessels containing the bones of the dead were set singly or in groups into the lateral chamber or were buried in pits. Sometimes the bones appear to have been burned before their final interment.

Some interesting variations may be observed in the positions in which the corpses were deposited in the tombs. In the stone sarcophagi, the large cist graves, and in some of the simple pit graves the body was put in a fully extended position, with arms parallel to the sides. Flexed burials or burials in a crouching or sitting position are found in shaft tombs and, occasionally, in cist graves. In several cases the body was buried in a standing position, occupying a shallow niche at the bottom of a vertical shaft. Multiple pit burials have also been observed with several corpses lying in disorder as if heaped up without any thought to their position.

Grave offerings at San Agustín are not elaborate. In most cases they consist of a few pottery vessels, some necklace beads of stone, scraping tools, grinding stones, and, rarely, some small gold object. Practically all burials contain a number of small chips of obsidian, which seem to have had a specific symbolic significance. Small accumulations of charcoal are also frequent in burials.

In attempting to interpret this great variety of burial practices, several authors have suggested, if not affirmed, that the differences correspond in essence to the social stratification of the ancient inhabitants. Undoubtedly, some of the major tombs, such as the stone coffins or certain large cist graves located on conspicuous spots, may have been the burial places of prominent people, but otherwise there is no evidence that social stratification alone accounts for the differences in burial type. It is much more reasonable to suppose that, given the considerable span of time observed at San Agustín, the variations in funerary customs are mainly due to chronological differences. Most unfortunately, although hundreds of tombs have been excavated to date, their distinctive pottery associations have not been recorded in adequate detail, and no attempt at seriation has been made. If the exact correlations of certain pottery types with distinct burial types were known, it would be possible to cross-date the grave offerings with the datable pottery sequences excavated in stratified midden sites.

Although there is no denying that there are many graves at San Agustín, the often advanced theories that this region was essentially a necropolis, or that the life of the ancient inhabitants was centered predominantly on the "cult of the dead," seem to be rather romantic and far-fetched. In comparison with other aspects of culture—such as habitation sites, midden deposits, earthworks, and fields, all of which occupy very large areas—the burial sites are a minor feature, not at all disproportionate to the normal cycle of life and death in any community over centuries of occupation.

24　Mesita B, North Barrow. Group of columnar statues (no longer *in situ*).

Chapter Five   **The Sculptor's Art**

At first sight the vast profusion of sculptures and the marked divergences in style make it almost impossible to establish categories of form and expression. Each carving appears as a world in itself, different from all others in form and unique in conception. Slowly and tentatively, one begins to discern similarities, but as soon as they are grasped their usefulness recedes; they seem too irrelevant and vague. Soon they are replaced by new impressions of fleeting familiarity of this or that isolated trait perceived by the wandering eye.

Of course, there are forms and details of workmanship that seem to fall into groups, and it is precisely these groups we find described in most archaeological reports dealing with ancient San Agustín. But, to the archaeologist, these monuments are mere aspects of material culture and must be recorded as such, classified according to relative size and exact measurements, shape, and function. And so the reports speak of ceremonial sculptures, carved boulders, relief slabs, and biomorphic representations, simply enumerating and measuring, emphasizing certain traits while ignoring others, and elaborating finally upon such subjects as "monumentality," feline statues, and double figures, to conclude with vague interpretations of religious symbolism and the magical attributes of "gods" and "demons."

In our appreciation of San Agustín stone sculpture we must go beyond this descriptive stage and look at the monuments as sculpture, as an artistic expression of a people—or peoples—whose aesthetic norms were, quite obviously, wholly different from ours, but whose creative endeavour, channeled by tradition, nevertheless produced a patterned image whose underlying form and content we must try to discover.[1]

Most San Agustín stone carvings consist of freestanding statues that are found, singly or in groups, on hilltops, on slopes, or in underground constructions. Within this class there are about half a dozen easily distinguishable categories. The first is represented by what will be designated here as columnar statues, consisting of a short cylindrical body with a rounded head, the sides carved very superficially to suggest a human figure (Plate 25). The next category, designated as flat statues, comprises elongated blocks of varying size with a more or less elliptical cross-section; these blocks have been carved in the shape of a human or near-human being, the frontal and dorsal views showing the carved contours, but the side view being flattened and disproportionate (Plate 35).

Another group consists of three-dimensional statues, carved fully in the round, and with an approximately circular cross-section (Plate 14). An important variant consists of elongated shaft-shaped stones with a square or wedge-shaped cross-section, representing a human or animal figure or both combined; on the flat sides, some of the details of these figures are projected in relief, a distinguishing characteristic of this type of sculpture (Plate 71). The category of small peg-shaped statues includes a large number of minor stone carvings representing human or near-human shapes, sometimes showing only the upper part of the body (Figure 7). The last group comprises isolated heads of varying sizes, some of human beings, others of fantastic creatures (Plate 26).

Another distinct class of San Agustín sculpture is formed by relief carvings on large elongated slabs. There are essentially two categories: slabs that were meant to stand upright, which generally represent anthropomorphic creatures, carved on both flat surfaces in frontal and dorsal views; and slabs that served as tomb covers or lids of sarcophagi, which are carved on the upper side only. The former generally show the contours of the figure, while the latter are often straight-sided, the upper surface forming an elongated square, or somewhat elliptical, panel on which the relief is carved (Plate 67).

Finally, there are the boulder carvings. Some are full carvings in which an entire, more or less rounded but essentially horizontal, boulder has been sculptured into a single or composite shape, generally that of a crouching animal or a group consisting of animal and human figures (Plate 30). Others are carved in low or high relief and use only part of

25 (far left)   Mesita B, North Barrow. Columnar statue.

26 (left)   La Estrella. Carved head.

27   Mesita B. Badly eroded columnar statue.

28   Mesita B. Feline columnar statue.

Fig. 7   Mesita A. Small peg shaped statue with feline features.

29   Mesita B, South Barrow. Two guardian figures.

the surface of the boulder (Plate 68). Bedrock carvings consist of flat rock formations in a riverbed that have been carved into diverse shapes, partly submerged in water (Plate 91).

The foregoing summary is, of course, nothing more than a generalized view of San Agustín's sculpture. I will now consider these works in greater detail and discuss first of all their principal formal elements. What immediately strikes the observer is the characteristic manner in which the native artist has handled the concept of volume. This refers not to mass, the mere physical quantity of matter, but to the configuration of a three-dimensional body in space, regardless of its size or weight. San Agustín sculpture consists of solid volumes that displace space without entering into any other relationship with it. Each sculpture is an isolated solid block without voids, without any internal spaces; thus it conveys an overwhelming impression of heavy squareness and compactness that is quite independent of its actual size. Even the flat statues or carved slabs give this impression. The sculptor never attempted to isolate part of his work, to detach it from its cylindrical or cuboid center, but always maintained this closed volume by working around it, so to speak, never trying to penetrate into it; when spaces occur, they are hardly more than gaps between two solid forms.[2]

Another salient feature is the infrequency of sculptures consisting of more than one component. In those that do, the secondary volumes are either closely integrated into the total sculpture or serve to emphasize the heaviness and solid mass of the primary one. This is the case, for example, in some of the statues with "doubles," in which a human figure is topped by a heavy cylindrical volume (Plate 63). Although the different volumes of the body—head, torso, legs, and so forth— are distinguished, the human figure is conceived not as a structure of

articulated parts but, rather, as a single volume. Moreover, there is no concern at all with anatomical details, except in some very minor traits.

It is characteristic of San Agustín figures that the internal proportions almost always show an oversize head, often representing a third or more of the total height of the statue. The volume of the head is frequently augmented by a headdress or helmet, while clothing, although occasionally present, does little or nothing to accentuate the volume of body parts. Another important trait is represented by the proportional relations among facial features, extremities, and decorative details. In many statues the mouth is the most elaborate anatomical part, with eyes, nose, and hands following in importance, while the neck, arms, and legs are of little sculptural concern.

This internal structure of all sculptural manifestations is, of course, closely related to the manner in which the artist conceived the visual qualities of the surface of his work. The square, blocklike appearance of most San Agustín sculpture implies, in many cases, the use of plane surfaces or, in the case of basically cylindrical volumes, the use of single-curved ones, either of which tends to enforce the flat, enclosed aspect of this art. The column or slab-shaped sculptures are simple solids bounded by essentially ruled surfaces that express a massive sense of immobility. This is true of most freestanding statues and also of the flat relief carvings, which—with rare exceptions—contain little beyond the surface that would suggest an internal dynamic structure. The boulder carvings, on the other hand, make use of double-curved surfaces that produce a roundness quite different from all other sculptures. It is this combination of double-curved surfaces that gives such sculptures as the eagle (Plate 32) and the toad (Plate 30) their roundness; indeed, their shapes suggest an internal power that makes these sculptures swell and almost burst as if an expanding

30 (below left) Matanzas. Large boulder carving of toad

31 Ullumbe. Boulder carving showing jaguar overpowering woman.

organic energy were pushing them outward. However, even these sculptures lack highlines or protuberances on their surfaces that would provide focal points of tension; their power lies exclusively in the sagging heaviness of their wide curvatures and in the crouching tension of their internal proportions.

I mentioned before that San Agustín sculpture consists of almost completely solid single-volume carvings, and I can add that this, of course, limits the expressive qualities of the statues. Even the use of concave surfaces is relatively restricted, in part because of the predominantly flat conception of all sculptural art. Their importance, however, in the play of shadows (which give expression to sculptural form) was recognized by the artist, who occasionally marked a jutting jaw, a staring eye, or a towering headdress with sweeping hollows that bring out deep shadows under the brow or nose, or set off a head from a body. The brooding, otherworldly expression so frequent in San Agustín sculpture is greatly enhanced by this device; nevertheless, these cavities never form truly important internal spaces.

In San Agustín sculpture there are no transitional shapes, no flowing lines of convex-concave surfaces that would blend one part of the body

61

32   Mesita B, Northwest Barrow. Statue of eagle holding snake.

33 Mesita A, East Barrow. Two guardian figures that probably flanked the
large statue in the center of the barrow.

into another in a smooth continuity of form and outline. The intersections
are brusquely marked by deep-cut grooves, and these sharp linear divisions
of body volumes are very characteristic of the inarticulate rigidity of
most sculptures. The head of a figure, often as wide as the body, from
which it is separated simply by a straight or curved groove, usually rests
squarely upon the hunched shoulders, and only in very few sculptures
does the neck appear as a transitional element between two major volumes.
If the hands are set off from the forearms, the chest from the abdomen,
or the feet from the legs, this is done more by the indication of adornment, such as ligatures, belts, or strings of beads, than by making any
concession to anatomical detail.

The schemata for the representation of the human body are essentially
the same in three-dimensional sculpture and in relief carving. An almost
straight-sided trunk, with high, square shoulders, is topped by an enormous head that is generally the most elaborately adorned part of the
statue, often being topped by a large and heavy headdress. The thin,
flat arms hang down or are bent stiffly at the elbows, the hands clutching
an object with ill-defined fingers or simply meeting over the chest,
empty and in a rigid pose. The legs and feet are barely outlined, and the
whole figure appears to lean slightly forward because of the hunched
shoulders. Otherwise, the body hardly ever expresses movement or
emotion. It is in the face, in the huge eyes and the grim mouth, that
expressive force is concentrated in all its brooding fierceness. The body
seems to be a mere base meant to sustain the head with its masklike face,
which is the true focal point of the sculpture.

63

Fig. 8   Mesita A. Small peg-shaped statue.

There can be no doubt that this particular schema for the composition of the human or near-human figure is an intentionally elaborated aspect of San Agustín art. It is of interest, then, to observe two closely related compositional features: axes and planes of reference. As seen from the front, the near absence of a neck gives the impression that the statues have a straight vertical axis, but a side view quite often shows that the head is slightly thrust forward, its axis at an angle to that of the trunk. Combined with the heavy, hunched shoulders, this protrusion, especially of the jaw, gives the statues a menacing lurch, which obviously was the sculptor's intention. The contracted arms and stocky legs emphasize this stooping, crouching pose. The majority of the statues are structured—or, rather, packed—around a single axis, in a more or less bilaterally symmetrical composition, and even those statues that express movement, such as those of the tomb guardians (Plate 16) and the one with the V-shaped chest mark (Plate 34), show this axial rigidity, their movements rotating around a vertical axis but never appearing excentric or freeing themselves from the immobility of the total volume. The arrangement, therefore, is always one of the utmost rigidity, which even violently menacing gestures cannot penetrate. In the aforementioned examples (Plates 16 and 34) the San Agustín sculptors had partly surmounted the technical obstacles of representing a body in movement; nevertheless, they always controlled

34 Mesita B, South Barrow. Statue with V-shaped chestmark.

this movement in a vertical, almost spiral, surge that only adds to the powerful impression these statues give.

The block-bound quality of the sculptures, together with the solid grouping of volumes along a single axis and the frequent use of plane surfaces, leads inevitably to a marked frontality. All component parts of a statue face in the same direction, and this orientation conveys the impression of watchful immobility, of a tense rigidity dominating every sculptural detail. It seems that most, if not all, San Agustín sculptures were intended to be viewed only from the front, and even such statues as are carved fully in the round display this frontality. In this connection it is of interest to call attention to several flat-sided sculptures, the different planes of which show the details of body form outlined in an orthographic projection. An example is the carving of a rodent (Plate 45), represented on a rectangular shaft on whose sides the contours of the body and limbs are delineated, the head being the only part carved in the round. Two more complex examples are the shaft-shaped sculptures shown in Plates 71 and 75, representing compositions of near-human and fantastic figures. The flat lateral surfaces bear the relief outlines of body parts in projection, while the narrow front view shows a rigid vertical composition in which the shoulders, hands, and legs are projected on planes that lie at right angles. In all three cases the sculptures are

65

35 and 36 Alto de las Piedras. Guardian statue with "double" and (right) detail of the head.

conceived not as true statues in the round but as four-sided reliefs with various two-dimensional planes and planimetric projections.

San Agustín statues rarely have human proportions. The body is blocked out in disregard of the natural internal proportions between head and trunk, eyes and mouth, or trunk and legs. This certainly is not attributable to the nature of the raw material the artist was using, since life-size elongated blocks are abundantly present. It was rather a conceptual schema that led the sculptor to compress organic forms into these top-heavy figures with oversize heads, squat bodies, contracted arms, and dwarfed legs.

Just as the freestanding statues never seem to extricate themselves wholly from the block, so the relief carvings are never quite released from their background but remain embedded in the surface of the slab. The artist's methods were more pictorial than sculptural, even in those carved slabs that were meant to have a statuesque quality. Many of the relief carvings seem to have been tomb covers representing the dead man or a tutelary spirit-being, and meant to be seen and used in a horizontal position, but many others were undoubtedly designed to stand upright and to be viewed from the front, having their edges carved—or rather, notched—to suggest the contours of the figure. The fact that most relief slabs were discovered lying on or in the ground does not constitute proof that they were not intended to stand vertically; indeed, the large statue still standing on the Alto de los Idolos (Plate 69) shows that these flat relief carvings were treated as freestanding images. There is, of course, a problem of physical stability. Having essentially short, cylindrical

66

shapes the three-dimensional freestanding sculptures are inherently stable, although the smaller ones, in which a heavy body volume is supported by slight, tapering legs, often had to be furnished with a broadened base. In fact, many of them include a base shaped like a flat square or circular plinth supporting the figure. The relief slabs, however, do not have these broadened bases, and it seems that their lower ends had to be buried deep in the ground to give them stability. As a result, the round figures have more of an earthbound quality than the relief slabs, which are far less closely related to the ground.

Some observations on the raw materials and technological processes of San Agustín sculpture are in order here. Almost all stone carvings are made of local volcanic materials: micaceous dacite, andesite, and feldspathic basalt, all of them fairly compact and hard rocks of a grayish or slightly yellowish color. Because the Pre-Columbian sculptors did not have metal tools, it is obvious that stone tools had to be used in the execution of their art, a painfully slow process that naturally imposed many limitations on both artist and craftsman. Some chisel-like tools have been found at San Agustín, but they seem to have been used in wood-carving or similar tasks, not for working with stone. The sculptor's technique probably consisted of the following steps: A convenient natural block or slab was set up, and the over-all form of the carving was blocked out by heavy blows with smaller stones. A schematic outline of the figure was then scratched onto one or more planes. Using a large number of heavy stone mauls, the sculptor pounded away at the surface with

37   Alto de las Piedras. Statue representing woman.

perpendicular strokes, crushing and pulverizing selected outside areas and thus working slowly inward until the desired shape emerged. Figural or ornamental details were produced by a combination of pounding and pecking techniques, sometimes with the sawlike movement of a straight-edged stone blade. The final step involved the application of abrasives in the form of different grades of crushed sand to polish the surfaces. These phases of the technical process can be observed on several statues, and it is apparent that surface-pecking, linear cutting, and massive abrasion were the principal means by which the stone sculptures were manufactured. Large numbers of fist-sized stone mauls have been found in close association with some of the statues, and the sculptured surfaces and planes show quite clearly the marks of innumerable pecking blows with which the surface was crushed and pounded away.[3]

The most difficult problem in analyzing the large number of stone carvings is, of course, that of style. Although most San Agustín sculptures represent basic forms pre-existing in nature, such as human or animal shapes, their execution is rarely naturalistic, showing instead a high degree of abstraction in terms of geometric simplification. Even if organic forms constitute the underlying perceptual models, these forms are interpreted, combined, and elaborated in a manner leading to the creation of entirely new beings that obviously existed only in the realm of imagination. The degree to which natural forms are carried to abstraction must be the focus of attention when trying to discern individual styles.

In our attempt to define styles we must examine the sculptures comparatively and seek those conventions of form, technique, and expression that are more or less stable and are common to a group of carvings. Rudimentary features and an over-all impression of unwieldy coarseness seem to justify the general denomination "archaic style" for the columnar statues of San Agustín. The entire carving is more a relief outline than a true sculpture, and one might suggest that this group of statues represents an initial stage of stone sculpture, probably derived from woodcarvings based on the natural shape of a tree trunk. These columnar carvings appear to be concentrated mainly in the Mesitas site and its immediate surroundings.[4]

Another stylistic group comprises a large number of freestanding statues and flat relief carvings that represent what I call the "expressionistic style." This group includes many of the major art works of ancient San Agustín. Their outstanding characteristics are hypertrophy of the head, combination of human and animal traits in the facial features, frontality enhanced by the near symmetry of the posture of the hands (which often carry objects), and elaborate headdress. The iconographic theme is almost always the jaguar-monster, a heavily compressed human body with an enormous head whose composite features—bared fangs, glaring eyes, and flaring nostrils—represent a snarling feline. The posture of the body itself expresses the crouching, menacing force contained in this being. The tightly contracted arms and the short, powerful legs convey a mood of taut, aggressive power. Even in those rare statues that lack the feline snout, the remaining features bear this grim, threatening expression. It was obviously the sculptor's intention not so much to make

69

38 El Tablon. Female statue with feline features.

39 (right) Mesita C. Statue with elaborate headdress.

a jaguar into a man as the reverse. The body, no matter how distorted or compressed, is essentially human; the arms terminate in fingers, not claws, and the legs, however shortened, are human legs. Even eyes and ears are humanoid, although the former vary widely in shape and often have a catlike slant. The short, stubby nose, with its flaring nostrils, although quite out of proportion, is more human than animal, and so are the deep furrows that often separate the mouth from the cheeks. Although all these features are grotesquely deformed and exaggerated they are conceptually human. But by their very exaggeration they blend easily with the bestial mouth into a dreadful, nonhuman face.

I turn once more to the initial classification of sculptures presented at the beginning of this chapter and consider first of all the general category of freestanding statues. The columnar statues obviously form a class apart, showing extremely crude representations of the human body combined with a head exhibiting marked animal features. The entire figure is tightly compressed into a cylindrical shape, no legs are indicated at all, and the stiff arms are merely outlined, quite often one arm hanging parallel to the body while the other is bent at a right angle, with the hand grasping the elbow of the other arm. The fingers are indicated by a

series of straight parallel grooves. The rounded head is frequently topped by a low cylindrical or blocklike extension;[5] the nose is broad and flattened and below it is a wide mouth or snout showing rows of teeth and four large pointed fangs. Statues such as the two stooping guardian figures (Plate 31) are closely related to this group, as are some of the small peg-shaped sculptures. The individual characteristics these statues have in common are an elongated cylindrical shape; absence of the lower extremities; a rounded head, frequently with an extension; round, protuberant eyes; a flat nose; a very broad and slightly grinning mouth with numerous square teeth and four triangular fangs; and thin, flat arms ending in parallel fingers. Moreover, all display an absence of decorative detail, a superficial groove technique, and a rough, pitted surface.

Details of dress and ornament are shown on many of these statues and consist of a variety of aprons, skirts, corded belts, ligatures, wristlets, elaborate headdresses, and broad necklaces that cover a great part of the torso. Large ear plugs or nose ornaments are present in some statues, and occasionally the hair or a close-fitting cap seems to be indicated by a horizontal or stepped line. A wide variety of headdresses are shown: some are similar to a visored or peaked cap; others are like a helmet, turban,

◁ 40 Naranjo. Feline statue.

41 Mesita B, South Barrow. Statue with conical headdress.

42 Mesita B, South Barrow. Statue holding fish.

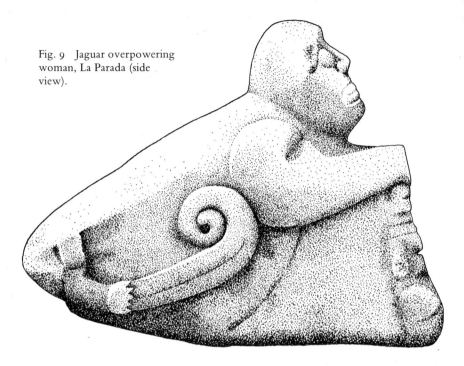

Fig. 9 Jaguar overpowering woman, La Parada (side view).

or caul. A twisted cord may encircle the head, while some statues appear to wear large feather crowns. At times the knots of certain cords are shown in considerable sculptural detail.[6]

In the characteristic hand-to-breast position, the hands are sometimes empty, but more often they hold an indeterminate object, vaguely in the shape of a staff or scepter. One figure carries a fish (Plate 42); another, a snake (Plate 65); and still another holds a cup in one hand (Plate 43). All, of course, represent human attitudes and man-made objects or symbols in animal shape, clearly demonstrating the essentially human origin of these beings. Abstraction and realism, imagination and naturalistic detail are thus combined in this style, which—notwithstanding its many different manifestations—does not lack a certain "classical" discipline.

A limited number of San Agustín stone carvings can be said to represent a "naturalistic style." In them the ambiguity of forms is wholly absent because the sculptor took animal or human shapes for his models without ever fusing their attributes. Most of these sculptures are boulder carvings or freestanding figures, the former representing animals and the latter human beings. Although each is readily recognizable by its shape and pose, these sculptures are not naturalistic in the sense that they try to imitate nature; they invariably simplify or emphasize certain traits, but always within the limits of the characteristics of a given species. The large sculptures depicting a bird of prey holding a snake (Plate 32) are good examples of this style. The hypertrophied head and the short, square legs immediately remind one of the expressionistic composite statues, but otherwise these unadorned animal sculptures represent an altogether different dimension, one of natural beings that lack the more sinister attributes of the jaguar-monster and have a quality of immediacy

Fig. 10 As Fig. 9 (front view).

Fig. 11 Statue of crouching woman, Quinchana.

quite absent in all other stylistic groups. However, these huge birds or toads, packed so tightly into their stony matrix, convey the same impression of a powerful pent-up force that we find in most of the ambiguous beings. The schema of the contracted limbs, updrawn shoulders, and large, neckless heads with round eyes applies also to the animal world.

Two or three composite sculptures, each of them showing a jaguar overpowering a smaller figure, can be included here. The first group (Plate 31) is very roughly blocked out of a massive dark-colored boulder from whose heavy volume the figures have not wholly extricated themselves. The second group (Figure 9) is more freely conceived and shows greater detail; the minor figure is of human shape, and the jaguar clutches between its paws a small childlike figure lying across the head of the one beneath it. Still more simplified quadrupeds combined with a subjacent figure are shown on some boulders, but often these are badly weathered and their contours blurred.

Realistic human sculptures are represented by the so-called guardian statues that flank the barrows containing subterranean chambers at the Mesitas site (Plate 16). The faces of these armed figures are carved in a much more realistic way than those of the monsters represented in other styles, the most striking difference being their small slitlike mouths. These figures are clearly not otherworldly beings. The stiffly defiant stance and the naturalism of their posture convincingly express the threat implied by their uplifted clubs—a menace quite different from that represented by the fangs of the jaguar-monster. The creatures crouching or hanging over the cylindrical extensions atop these statues are in the archaic style, and their heavy volumes enhance the forceful and realistic movements of the statues. The female figure from Quinchana (Figure 11)

75

is another example of the naturalistic style. Shown in a sitting posture, with her hands touching her knees and her face turned slightly upward, she conveys an expression of expectant awareness that is wholly human. An element of realism is indicated by the simple angular line delineating the sagging breasts. The figure in Plate 43 also shows marked traits of realism, especially in the sculptural treatment of the face. In addition, two relief-carved slabs (Plate 44 and Figure 15) that were used to cover sarcophagi show a certain degree of naturalism, even in body proportions.

The next category is the "abstract style." It includes a number of sculptures in which the simplification of human or animal forms has reached a high degree of abstraction. Plate 46 shows an example in which a series of square angular volumes and planes has been balanced by another set of rounded ones. A square trunk and elliptical head, square arms and rounded bracelets, square eyes and rounded ears, a square stepped frontline and a rounded chin—all combine into a coherent and expressive structure, a powerful geometric design of blank remoteness. A similar statue is shown in Plate 47, while an entirely different form of abstraction can be seen in Plate 48, which shows a human torso whose lower part is covered by a winged and stepped design,[7] while the head is conceived as a broad angular block upon which the face is projected in three planes. The eyes are traced as spirals that contrast

43 Alto de los Idolos. Female statue with cup.

44 Alto de los Idolos. Four-sided relief carving.

45 Naranjos. Statue of crouching woman.

with the square, boxlike mouth. Similar in conception is a statue from whose mouth protrudes a slablike body ending in a head (Plate 78). The statues shown in Plate 50 and in Figure 16, one of a jaguar-monster and the other of an isolated jaguar head, are very similar in that both combine sweeping volutes, spirals and circles with square and triangular elements into a flowing abstract design. A remarkable statue is illustrated in Plate 34: the body parts are outlined in heavy square volumes that alternate with deep-set triangular shapes, while the broad curve of the headdress is echoed by the incised scroll designs covering the chest and the forehead. Another juxtaposition of squares and curves can be seen in the statue shown in Plate 49. Also belonging to this same stylistic group is the boulder relief carving in Plate 85.

46 Quebradillas. Statue with masklike face.

47   Ullumbe. Statue with masklike face.

48   El Batán. Statue with spiral-shaped eyes.

49   Alto de Lavaderos. Statue with hands on shoulders.

50 Unknown provenance. Statue with bag.

It is obvious that none of the major styles outlined above constitutes
clearly delimitable units in form and expression and that there exist
intermediate forms that represent either transitional points in an internal
development or outside influences that perhaps did not spread sufficiently
to be more widely accepted. The "Gothic" mode displayed by the statue
shown in Plate 87 provides such an example, as do a number of other
statues and relief carvings.

51   Mesita C. Statue with triangular head.

Chapter Six   **The World of the Jaguar-Monster**

The stone sculptures of San Agustín obviously express an aspect of the
religious ideas and experiences of the native peoples who had established
themselves in this region in prehistoric times, and we must turn now to
the difficult task of trying to interpret these images in terms of their
cultural background and symbolic significance.

We can easily deduce that the statues served different functions, some
of them as public monuments, others buried as part of a funerary ritual.
The first category appears to include two forms: statues found within a
sepulchral chamber or tomb, which—because of this specific location—
we can suppose to have been important sacred images, and statues, slabs,
or carved boulders found out of doors and not necessarily associated with
burial practices. No matter what the location of the statues may be, and
regardless of their particular stylistic qualities, it is evident that most
sculptures incorporate a single underlying theme, that of the jaguar-
monster, which is expressed in a wide range of forms. There can be no
doubt that this iconographic motif of a man turned into a ferocious
feline creature is predominant and that it has a remarkable continuity
in time, having persisted for centuries and perhaps millennia.

In most cases the jaguar-monster is represented as a single, isolated
creature. We can recognize it as such in the columnar statues of the
archaic style, as well as in many statues and carved slabs of the expressionistic and abstract styles. In the expressionistic sculptures especially, this
creature often carries specific attributes in its hands: scepter-like staffs,
small unidentified objects, and occasionally a fish or snake. Other sculptures of this feline type show group scenes: the monster is portrayed with
other figures that are integrated as secondary elements into the total
image, as in the large boulder sculptures executed in the naturalistic
style. In both of these categories a jaguar, devoid of human characteristics, is shown in the act of overpowering a smaller figure, which in all
probability represents a human being. Until quite recently only the
sculpture from the Ullumbe site (Plate 31) had been known, and designated the "monkey group" by Preuss—a term that has found its place
ever since in archaeological literature.[1] It is true that this sculpture is very
coarse and badly weathered, making it difficult to identify, but it is also
quite evident that the main figure has a broad head and a snout with
clearly outlined teeth, features very unlike those of a monkey. What
induced Preuss to interpret this sculpture as a monkey was undoubtedly

52   Mesita B, Northwest Barrow. Statue with triangular headdress.

the tail, which lies on the figure's back with its end coiled into a spiral, a position that naturally reminds one of the prehensile tails of New World monkeys. However, in the light of a recently discovered sculpture from the La Parada site (Figure 9), this interpretation must be revised. The latter sculpture, quite similar in composition and posture to the Ullumbe carving, represents, beyond any doubt, a jaguar that is overpowering a smaller, human figure with marked female characteristics (the circular earrings, small slitlike mouth, and headband are all repeated in other sculptures representing women). In addition, the jaguar grasps the small figure of a child, which lies on the female's back. Most important, however, is the fact that the jaguar's tail is coiled in a spiral, demonstrating that Preuss's interpretation of the first sculpture as a monkey was probably fallacious, this type of tail being that of a jaguar.[2]

We can speak, then, of three forms of feline representations: one in which a realistic jaguar attacks a human female; one in which a man acquires feline attributes and is partly transformed into a grotesque jaguar; and one in which a jaguar-man is associated with other monstrous beings, as in the statues shown in Plates 16 and 75. From the point of view of conceptualization, workmanship, stylistic detail, and, perhaps, advanced weathering, it might be possible to suggest that the naturalistic style (which, as we have pointed out already, is closely related to archaic

84

sculptures) is older than the expressionistic and the abstract and that the composite statues are a late elaboration of the jaguar-monster motif. What, then, do these different types of feline sculptures represent, and how do they express iconographically one of the major tenets of a religious system?

This question is difficult to answer. The best we can do in attempting to solve it is to discuss certain parallels that come to mind. In the first place, representations of feline monsters are a recurrent motif in prehistoric aboriginal art, especially in the so-called Nuclear American area, the cultural heartland of native developments, which stretches from Mexico to Chile. The feline monster is represented here in pottery and textiles, in metal or in jade, in carved wood or in large stone sculptures, in pictographs and petroglyphs, and ranges over an enormous area and thousands of years of cultural continuity, it being the central motif of an art that obviously expresses a deep-rooted religious idea.[3] Moreover, the jaguar looms large in aboriginal mythology and folklore, already in the early texts gathered by the first Spanish chroniclers, as well as in the ethnological literature dealing with historical or extant tribal societies.[4]

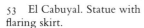
53   El Cabuyal. Statue with flaring skirt.

Let us for the moment pass over the possible reasons why the natives should have chosen this particular beast to express their religious ideas, and consider only the evidence provided by archaeology. There can be no doubt that the so-called feline cult is a very ancient element in American Indian cultures. It probably goes back to the early hunters who, thousands of years ago, peopled the Western Hemisphere; its first origins lie in the Old World, on the cultural level of palaeolithic societies. In America, its earliest appearance as an elaborate ideological system, expressed in well-defined iconography, occurs in the Olmec culture, the oldest civilization of the New World, which flourished near the Gulf of Mexico in what is today the region of Veracruz. Olmec culture expressed many of its religious concepts in gigantic stone sculptures, and the monuments discovered thus far present a wide range of images, among which the jaguar motif is of prime importance. The principal representations consist of human beings with feline features indicated mainly by a snarling muzzle or snout, of more realistic jaguar images, sometimes shown attacking a person, and of the ubiquitous figure of a small, large-headed child on whose puffy face the feline traits are marked in a very characteristic way. The culture that produced these stone images flourished roughly between 1200 and 400 B.C. and exercised a wide and lasting influence upon all major cultural developments in the Mesoamerican area. Stylistically, Olmec sculpture is entirely different from anything discovered so far in South America, but what interests us here is the underlying idea of a jaguar-spirit or -monster, a thread we shall try to follow in some of its ramifications. We shall examine briefly several aspects of this religious system, which—because of its early position in time and its strongly formalized iconography—provides an important starting point for any discussion concerned with the jaguar cult.[5]

Among the Olmec stone monuments is one of special importance discovered in the region of Potrero Nuevo, Veracruz, by Dr. Matthew W. Stirling of the Smithsonian Institution. Stirling, who described it as representing a jaguar copulating with a woman, commented: "The episode represented must have been an important feature of Olmec mythology. It is particularly interesting in view of the frequent representation of part human and part jaguar figures in Olmec art."[6] The parallel with the two San Agustín sculptures mentioned above is a very striking one because the Olmec stone carving is virtually identical with the carvings showing a jaguar overpowering a woman. The similarity refers, of course, not to any stylistic resemblances but exclusively to a common theme—the idea of a powerful feline that enters into a direct relationship with a member of the human species, thus establishing a bond that leads eventually to a close and permanent association of a sacred or, at least, otherworldly character. We must look then for other parallels of this kind and consider the nature of this strange man-animal relationship.

The close association between shamanism and jaguar-spirits is another widespread complex in American aboriginal cultures, and an abundant literature exists on this subject. Stated briefly, the basic idea is that the shaman or witch doctor can turn into a jaguar at will, using the form of

54 Alto de Lavaderos. Statue
representing seated figure.

this animal as a disguise, sometimes in order to achieve beneficial ends,
sometimes to threaten or to kill. The jaguar appears as a helper and a
friend of the shaman's, lending not only his exterior form but also his
power—natural or supernatural—to the shaman's quest. Eventually,
after death, the shaman turns permanently into a jaguar and can manifest
himself in this form to the living, again in a beneficial or maleficent way,
as the case may be. These or similar ideas have been known to prevail
among many Indian tribes, especially those of the South American tropics,
but they are by no means unknown in the more advanced Andean cultures. In the Mesoamerican area the same relationship between the
jaguar and the shaman has been observed, and, even on the level of
elaborately structured belief systems and an institutionalized priesthood,
the jaguar plays an important role as a supernatural helper or avenger.
From this association the concept of the were-jaguar, or *nahual*, has
arisen, the feline monster with supernatural powers or, in reverse, the
shaman with feline attributes. We shall return to this point later; for the
moment it must suffice to call attention to this ancient and widespread
association of ideas.

55   Mesita D. Statue of pot-bellied jaguar.

56   Mesita B, Northwest Barrow. Detail of statue.

57 Mesita C. Statue with squared
mouth.

58 Alto de los Idolos, West
Barrow. Main statue.

59 and 60 Mesita B, Northwest Barrow. Statue with head trophy and (right) detail of head.

We can now narrow down our field of inquiry to the local scene. In Colombian archaeology the jaguar motif is found in many different cultural contexts and in diverse eras, going back at least to the beginning of the first millennium B.C. Pottery representations of fanged feline creatures first appear in the context of small farming villages[7] and continue, from then on, in many forms, sometimes in clay and small stone carvings and eventually in gold objects. The main center of elaborate jaguar representations is undoubtedly San Agustín, but the motif also appears in the minor arts of the Tairona area of northern Colombia, in the Chibcha highlands, in the central provinces, and on the southern Pacific Coast.[8] This distribution is certainly not complete, because many prehistoric representations were very probably made in perishable materials such as wood, bone, textiles, or bark-cloth; there seems to have been an especially great number of large ceremonial wood carvings.[9] As a matter of fact, the Spanish chroniclers of the early sixteenth century frequently referred to large wooden images, generally associated with temples or other ceremonial sites, and often facing the east. An explicit example is contained in an account by Pedro Cieza de León, an eyewitness

to the conquest of the Cauca Valley tribes about 1540, who wrote that the Indians of Caramanta, a region to the northwest of San Agustín, had in their temples "certain boards in which they carve the figure of the devil, very fierce, and in human form, with other idols and figures of cats which they worship."[10] The jaguar-monster also played an important part among the ancient Indians of the northern provinces; among the Indians of the chiefdoms of Guaca, "the devil appeared in the form of a very fierce tiger."[11] The same was reported in early Spanish sources from the chiefdoms of Sinú, Nutibara, and others: The shamans and priests who officiated in these temples were said to "speak with the devil," consulting him or receiving his orders. Of the Guayupe, a tropical rain-forest tribe that in the sixteenth century lived to the northeast of San Agustín, the chronicles reported that their shamans turn into jaguars at will,[12] the jaguar-spirit always being closely associated with shamanistic practices.

Among many Indian tribes that survive at present in Colombia, the jaguar continues to occupy an important position in myths, shamanistic rituals, and individual beliefs, and even among the Spanish-speaking peasants it is sometimes thought that a local witch doctor may turn into a jaguar in order to commit evil deeds. Among the Kogi Indians of the Sierra Nevada the myths tell of huge, ferocious jaguars that, at the beginning of time, were born of the Universal Mother, and of the Jaguar-People, who were the descendants of this mythical race and at the same time the direct ancestors of the modern Kogi. There are many myths and traditions recounting the exploits of different jaguar personifications, and of all these ancestral spirit-beings it is said that they were great shamans who were able to change freely from human to animal form and back again, establishing rituals, fighting wars, and exercising their dominion over all the mountains. The Kogi still use elaborately carved wooden masks representing the jaguar-monster, and during certain ceremonial dances their songs are addressed to this personification of supernatural power.[13] Among the Chimila, Noanamá, Embérá, Catío, Tunebo, and many tribes of the Orinoco plain, the jaguar is an important spirit-being, always connected with shamanistic ritual and belief. The rain forests of the Northwest Amazon (which include the Vaupés, Caquetá, and Putumayo regions) constitute another immense area in which the jaguar plays an important role in tribal beliefs. Among the Tukanoan tribes—both their eastern and western groups—as well as among the Witoto and their neighbors, shamans are believed to turn into jaguars, and many myths and rituals refer in detail to the powers and supernatural attributes of these beasts.[14]

Not far from San Agustín, in the region of Tierradentro, a mountainous district at the headwaters of the Cauca River, several thousand Páez Indians still live; this Chibcha-speaking tribe, although fairly acculturated in some respects, conserves many traits of the ancient aboriginal belief system. Given the close proximity of this large tribe to the San Agustín region, its body of living traditions is of extraordinary interest in relation to our discussion. In the beginning of time, according to Páez mythology, a young Indian woman was raped by a jaguar, and from this union the

61 and 62   Mesita B, Northwest Barrow. Two views
of guardian statue with "double."

63   Mesita B, Northwest Barrow. Guardian statue
"double."

Thunder-Jaguar was born. The child grew up into a man, who became an important cultural hero and eventually retired to a lagoon in the mountains, where his spirit continued to dwell. Thunder is the central theme of all Páez myths and is closely associated with the concepts of fertility, the jaguar-spirit, and shamanism. As a matter of fact, a prospective shaman receives the supernatural call to his office from Thunder, and it is near a lagoon that his apprenticeship takes place, accompanied by visionary, hallucinatory experiences. A Páez shaman can turn into Thunder, and evil shamans can turn into jaguars in order to steal cattle or sheep. According to the myths the Thunder-Jaguar has many children who occasionally appear in a miraculous manner and become the shaman's helpers. These Thunder-Children are voracious creatures, each of them having several female servants—young girls whom they kill by drinking

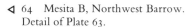

◁ 64   Mesita B, Northwest Barrow.
Detail of Plate 63.

65   Mesita B, South Barrow. Statue holding snake.

their blood and milk. When these Thunder-Children appear in a shaman's vision they display their male organs ostentatiously and, once they become of age, they steal women and carry them off to their dwellings at the bottom of the lagoons. There are many tales of shamans turning into jaguars and of fights among the Thunder-People as they try to wrest from each other golden staffs and other power symbols.[15]

A recent event among the modern Páez illustrates well their attitudes toward the powerful feline. In the vicinity of the village of Mosoco the Indians killed a large puma that was playing havoc with the livestock. The dead animal was carried triumphantly to the village where, in one of the houses, its body was laid out on a sort of altar crowned by an elaborate arch of branches beneath which the beast was put in a lifelike crouching position and surrounded by candles. The room and altar were adorned with flowers and red cloth, and the people danced around it, playing their musical instruments. At last the carcass was butchered, and each participant in the celebration was given a small morsel to eat but not before being warned that the meat should be prepared without the addition of salt.[16]

Fig. 12   Flat statue with circular eyes, Le Pelota.

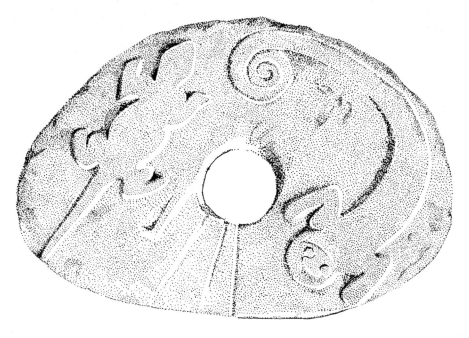

Fig. 13   Perforated slab with relief-carved reptiles, North Barrow of Mesita B;
now at El Batán.

This complex of ideas, found so close to the San Agustín region, acquires special significance and provides a body of information from which we can follow new directions of inquiry. In the first place, it is remarkable that the Páez creation myth should clearly describe the theme that I mentioned when speaking of Olmec sculpture: the rape of an Indian woman by a jaguar as the origin of a new race. Second, there are a number of additional motifs that bear discussion. The association, or, rather, identification, of the jaguar with thunder is here a point of interest. In the sixteenth century the temple of the great thunder deity Dabeiba, in northwestern Colombia, had a jaguar for a guardian.[17] Among the Kogi Indians the ancestral jaguar-spirit is often identified with thunder and lightning and, again, appears as the guardian of the ceremonial sites.[18] Similar associations are found among the Tukanoan tribes of the Northwest Amazon. The Desana creation myth says, "The Sun created the jaguar to be his representative on earth, he gave him the (yellow) color of his power and he gave him the voice of thunder which is the voice of the Sun."[19] In fact, the concept of a Thunder-Jaguar who represents the solar creator figure is common among these Indians.[20] I could go on and quote many more such associations, but we must return to the Páez traditions. From the description given above, it becomes clear that the power of the jaguar-monster has a very strong sexual component. First we learn of the sexual assault upon a young woman, and then we are told that her offspring display their sexual organs and, eventually, grow up to assault women whom they kill by voraciously drinking their blood and milk. This imagery corresponds closely to Kogi myths, according to which the mythical jaguar-monsters used to assault women, sometimes in the disguise of a shaman pretending to

97

effect a cure. A historical tradition, based on events that are said to have happened some three generations ago, tells of a Kogi girl who was attacked by a jaguar and bitten in the breast. The girl began to growl like a jaguar, died shortly after, and was buried. During the night the jaguar returned and devoured the corpse. The men killed the jaguar, and upon examining the body discovered that one of its paws was shaped like a human foot.[21]

66   Ullumbe. Statue with protruding tongue (?).

67 Mesita C. Statue with two staffs.

The Thunder-Jaguars of Páez mythology make us think again of the Olmec of the Gulf of Mexico. Dr. Michael D. Coe, an authority on the Olmec, emphasizes the childlike aspect of many of their sculptures: "The Olmec evidently believed that at some distant time in the past, a woman had cohabited with a jaguar, this union giving rise to a race of were-jaguars, combining the lineaments of felines and men. These monsters are usually shown in Olmec art as somewhat infantile through life, with puffy features of small, fat babies."[22] Another Olmec specialist, Miguel Covarrubias,[23] who studied in detail the stylistic developments of feline traits in these sculptures, demonstrated that such personifications were essentially rain spirits and the prototypes of the later rain gods of the Mesoamerican area. On the other hand, these ancestral jaguar-babies still survive in the folklore of the coast of Veracruz under the name of *chaneques*, dwarfed beings who live in cascades and who, besides being rain spirits, are said to persecute women.[24] It is evident that all these attributes make them appear closely related to the small Thunder-Jaguars of the Páez and to other spirit-beings prominent in Colombian Indian traditions. In the highlands of southern Colombia, a region contiguous with the San Agustín area, the local Indians believe in the existence

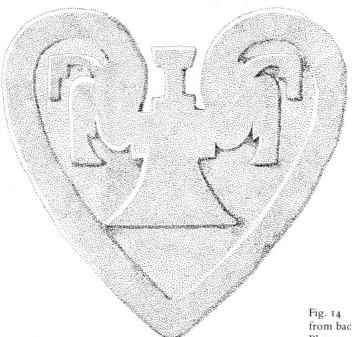

Fig. 14 Heart-shaped relief carving from back of statue illustrated in Plate 59.

of childlike spirits who live behind cascades in the rivers and are associated with the rainbow. They too persecute girls and women, sometimes appearing to them in sexual fantasies and causing them to waste away if not treated by a local shaman. When annoyed, they turn into jaguars and may attack a house, but then the men frighten them off by putting on masks and a dress of bark-cloth.

It is obvious, then, that all these traditions belong to the same sphere of aboriginal thought and symbolism. But the Mexican *chaneques* are also the supernatural masters of game animals and fish, and here a new parallel with Colombian Indian cultures arises. Among the Tukanoan tribes the supernatural Master of Animals is imagined as a red dwarf who dwells in caves or at the bottom of deep pools; he is closely associated with the jaguar, sexually assaults women and young girls, and watches over the fertility and increase of the animal world. It is from him that the shamans must obtain permission for the hunters and fishermen, who themselves have to obey the strict rules established by this supernatural gamekeeper.[25]

As we can see, this thread of ideas and associations is beginning to weave a colorful network. Jaguars, voracious little beings, and thunder combine with rain, fertility, and sexual aggression in a complex pattern of interrelated beliefs that constitute the principal sphere of most shaman-istic practices. We are beginning to move into a dimension of primitive thought that grows increasingly intricate as we continue our analysis.

The Colombian Indian shaman is characterized by many aspects of sexual energy that are partly derived from, and partly reflected upon, the spirit-beings or material objects that constitute his helpers or tools. Among practically all Tukanoan and Witotan tribes, the shaman and the jaguar are designated by a single term, a name derived from the Indian word for cohabitation (*ye'e*).[26] Both the man and the beast are seen as progenitors and procreators, as possessing great sexual power—the former representing society; the latter, nature. A shaman's apprenticeship is always accompanied by sexual abstinence, fasting, and purification, and special care is taken in avoiding certain condiments or other foods associated symbolically with sexual activities. Within the context of Tukanoan culture, sexual energies are concentrated in the shaman's person in terms of a powerful life force, to be freed and used by him for the benefit of his group only. His ceremonial adornment, an elongated cylinder of whitish quartz, is called the "Sun's penis";[27] his staff is the phallic world axis from which, according to myth, the Sun Creator's

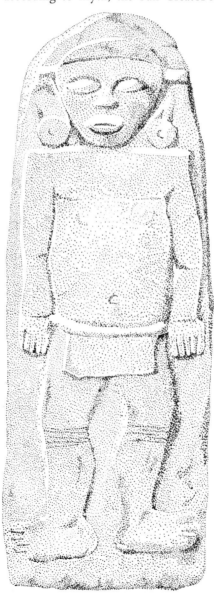

Fig. 15 Relief-carved lid of sarcophagus, Mesita B, Northwest Barrow.

68   El Cabuyal. Thick carved slab.

69   Alto de los Idolos. Carved slab.

70 (above right)   Mesita C. Carved slab.

sperm dripped down to the earth and brought into existence the first
men who peopled the land. But there is nothing salacious or erotic
about these concepts and attributes; in reality, they simply express a
profound consciousness of the life force, which gives continuity to
existence but has to be channeled and controlled if it is not to be destructive
to society or to the individual.

The jaguar, on the other hand, expresses this vital energy in nature.
According to the Indians, his roar is the roar of thunder that announces
the fertilizing rains; his color is the bright color of the east, of the rising
sun—the seminal color of creation and growth. His attribute is the
quartz and the rock-crystal, another symbol of seminal fluid, particles
of which are the thunderbolts the shaman collects at the spot where
lightning has struck. The jaguar is the guardian of the sib house, which
is imagined as a great protective womb over which he dominates with
his fertilizing power. The Tukano say, "Just as the Sun, with his power,
procreated the earth, so the jaguar is procreating, clad in his yellow coat.
Like a man dominating a woman."[28]

71–74 Alto de Lavapatas. Statue with "double" showing details from (left) rear, (below left) side, and (right) head.

Fig. 16   Carved head of
jaguar-monster, La Parada.

The jaguar is, then, essentially a power animal. This, of course, is true not only in American aboriginal cultures. But as a power symbol he is ambivalent, the male procreative energy easily becoming a destructive agent, profoundly affecting the delicate equilibrium of kinship and social relations at large. It is this ambivalent force the shaman has to master, and here lies the key to the close relationship between man and beast, between the shaman as a representative of society and the dark life forces he sees embodied in this powerful animal. According to the Indians, part of man's essence is of jaguar origin—a wild untrammeled energy, all-devouring in its impulses—and therefore the shaman has to tame the jaguar, has to become a jaguar himself in order to control and direct this energy into channels that will avoid harm to others.[29]

We must turn now to another most important aspect of shamanistic attitudes. I mentioned that among the Páez Indians a shaman receives his supernatural call from the Thunder-Jaguar during a visionary experience, and the same is true for the Tukanoan and other Colombian tribes. We must examine now in greater detail the origin and nature of these visions and the role they play in shamanistic and religious experience.

The use of hallucinogenic drugs derived from certain native plants is very widespread among Colombian Indians. A large number of different species are used to induce visions. One of the principal plants is a leguminous tree, *Anadenanthera peregrina* (also called *Piptadenia*), from which a narcotic snuff, generally called *yopo*, is obtained, containing the hallucinogenic substance bufoteine. Another common narcotic plant is the jungle vine of the genus *Banisteriopsis*, called commonly *yajé*, from different species of which a strong psychoactive drink is prepared. Still more widespread is the datura tree, source of another powerful hallucinogen. Many other plant substances, of minor importance, produce similar effects.[30]

From the available literature it is apparent that many, if not all, Colombian Indian religions were either based upon or closely related to the use of drug-induced hallucinations and that these altered states of consciousness provided an important mechanism for individual and collective supernatural experience. The sixteenth-century chronicler Pedro de Aguado made one of the earliest references to this fact when speaking of the use of *yopo* snuff and tobacco among the Guayupe Indians. Aguado said that the Indians "remain in a drowsiness in which the devil, in their dreams, shows them all the vanities and vices he wishes them to see, all of which they take for a most certain revelation." He went on to say:

This habit of taking *yopo* and tobacco is very common all over the New Kingdom and also, I understand, in most of the Indies . . . being the instrument and tool by which the devil takes advantage of them, because, as I said, with the smoke the Indians take of these two things they become intoxicated and are deprived of their natural reason, and it is thereby that the Fiend takes advantage to make them worship him and follow other misleading precepts he wishes to impose.[31]

Among the ancient Chibcha of the Bogotá highlands *yopo* and datura were commonly used by shamans and priests, and most references in the Spanish chronicles to Indian shamans' "speaking with the devil" or to the devil's appearing to them can be interpreted as an indication that hallucinogens were being used. The important fact is that in their preparation, and in the hallucinations induced by them, the imagery of the jaguar plays a major role. The objects used in connection with narcotic powers, such as snuffing tubes, tablets, mortars, or small containers, are often adorned with jaguar motifs, and many of these objects are of prehistoric origin, demonstrating the antiquity of this custom.[32] Among the western Tukanoan tribes of the headwaters of the Caquetá River, quite close to San Agustín, the men who drink a *Banisteriopsis* concoction claim to turn into jaguars and to pursue game;[33] the eastern Tukano and most Arawaken tribes of the Vaupés and Orinoco areas claim to see jaguars or to change into them. Among the Guahibo of the Vichada River the *yopo* powder is kept in a tubular jaguar bone, and the shaman, whose insignia are a crown of jaguar claws and a jaguar skin worn over his back, claims to turn into a jaguar under the effects of the drug.[34] Among the Páez, too, a plant is mentioned that permits its user to change into a jaguar.[35]

But this hallucinatory jaguar is ambivalent, as I have said. For some people who take the drugs, the jaguar appears as a threatening, horrifying image, a devouring monster, while to others he appears tame and subservient, a helper and a friend. The effect depends, of course, to a high degree upon the individual's personality and expectations and on the psychological and social atmosphere of the seance. It is also true that not all aboriginal tribes of Colombia have used or are using the powerful drugs described above. Projected upon the wavering screen of drug-induced hallucinations, enlarged and distorted, the image of the jaguar is certainly much more awesome than the one formed by those peoples who did not commonly use psychoactive drugs to alter their states of consciousness.

If we look again at the statues in the light of what has been said above, we shall be able to approach these figures of fantasy and nightmare in a new way. Within the context of hallucinatory experience and its continuity from prehistoric times to the present, San Agustín sculpture acquires a new meaning, and we can see it as an art that tried to give concrete expression to a complex system of ideas, the diverse threads and details of which we find in many other aboriginal cultures.

Some of the most impressive stone sculptures show a personage over whose back a monstrous feline crouches (Plate 75). The significance of these composite statues has often been discussed in the literature. Most authors have seen in them so-called *alter ego* representations—doubles or guardian spirits that accompany and protect people. This sculptural motif has been found in several regions of aboriginal America, notably in Central America and in the Amazon Basin.[36] It has recently been suggested that these *alter ego* carvings are probably connected with the use of psychoactive snuffs, the double motif and the jaguar being common

75 Alto de las Piedras. Statue with "double."

76   Alto de las Piedras. Detail of Plate 75.

features shown on the paraphernalia that are used in connection with these narcotics.[37] It has also been suggested that certain prehistoric jaguar effigies from Peru and Central America, in the form of stone mortars, were originally used in the preparation of these or similar drugs.[38] These comparisons, seen now within the context of feline imagery and shamanism, begin to throw an entirely new light upon the symbolic significance of these and other San Agustín sculptures and give to it a much wider meaning, in accordance with a broad underlying system of beliefs related to the shamanistic power quest and the all-important concept of procreative energy.

We must now turn briefly to some other aspects of San Agustín sculpture that are marginal to the jaguar motif but that in all probability are somehow related to it. Several large sculptures (Plate 30) depict toads, which figure prominently in aboriginal mythology and which, according to several Colombian tribes, symbolize the female principle. Among the Kogi Indians the word for toad (*maukuí*) is a common epithet for the female sex organ,[39] and a number of mythological toads are associated with diseases and other dangers.[40] In Kogi mythology the toad was an adulterous woman who was punished by her husband, the Sun; since then all toads have represented symbolically the female sex in an adulterous and aggressive sense.[41] Among the Tukanoan tribes a large

supernatural toad is mentioned that at night turns into a human being and devours certain ants, which have a marked masculine connotation, according to the Indians.[42]

Snakes and lizards appear occasionally in San Agustín sculpture, but they are not prominent motifs. The image of a large bird grasping a snake is represented in several sculptures (Plate 32) and probably depicts a crane-hawk (*Geranospiza caerulescens*), a bird that can often be seen catching snakes in this way. The hawk-snake motif is frequent in Indian mythology and sometimes refers symbolically to a dualistic opposition between life-bringing and life-destroying forces associated with the east and the west.

Several figures hold children in their arms (Plate 18). One of the largest feline representations holds a small childlike creature, its head hanging downward in what is not a protective pose (Plate 77). To try to interpret these sculptures would be merely to speculate, and the same applies to certain other figures that seem to devour an object or some creature protruding from their mouths (Plates 66, 78). Two feline statues display human skulls hanging from cords around their necks (Plate 59), and we are reminded of the head trophies taken by numerous Colombian tribes in the past, a custom described in considerable detail by the early Spanish chroniclers.

On some of the statues we can observe certain minor sculptural details that are repeated here and there and that probably had a specific iconographic significance now lost to us. Among them are the carefully

77 (left)   Mesita B,
Northwest Barrow.
Double statue holding
child.

78   Mesita B, South
Barrow. Statue holding
child.

79 El Tablon. Statue with nose ornament.

represented knots (Plates 14, 73, 75), a bird-shaped head ornament (Plate 56), and a twisted headband (Plate 79). On the composite statues showing doubles, it sometimes appears as if a skin, perhaps a jaguar's hide, was being represented as hanging over the back of the secondary figure (Plate 72). Some dragonlike creatures also appear on these statues, combined and entwined with the main figure (Plate 75). These motifs are probably elaborations of the jaguar motif or are attributes that begin to individualize some of its personifications—a development well documented from other parts of aboriginal America where the jaguar is a predominant theme. In San Agustín the jaguar-monster has in general remained simpler than in Mesoamerica or the Central Andes. Diversified as an individual experience and interpreted by the native artist, it still forms a unified motif expressing the fundamental range of ideas traced in the preceding pages.

The jaguar is the personification of fertility in the widest sense. The basic model is human procreation, with its phallic and seminal attributes; but in the broader scene of life the concept of fertility includes all cyclic growth—animals and plants, seasons and harvest, game for the hunter and crops for the farmer. Hence the chain of associations extends from sperm symbolized by crystals to thunder, rain, and the rising sun. But as procreation and fertility, originally patterned on the human model, are ambivalent (for they contain the seeds of aggression and social disruption), so too the jaguar appears as the symbolic expression of darkness and destruction, as the insatiable devourer.

It is obvious then that the jaguar-monster is not a deity, a divine being whom people would adore as a god, but rather a general principle of creation and destruction—a natural life force, so to speak—himself subject to a higher power. This point is clearly stated in many aboriginal myths: The jaguar was not alone in the beginning but was created by a divine being and sent into this world as a great ambivalent force capable of good or evil. It has to be mastered not only by the shaman but also by each person for himself, if a moral and social order is to be preserved. The jaguar is man, is the male; it stands for all human nature that is sexually and socially aggressive and predatory, and whose energy has to be curbed by cultural restrictions to ensure the survival of society.

80   Isnos Period. Double-spouted vessel.

Chapter Seven   **Pots, Stones and Chronology**

From what has been said in the preceding chapters, it is clear that San Agustín is an extensive archaeological area and that its cultural remains include a great variety of forms, of which stone monuments are only one. The geographical extension, as well as the marked stylistic differences in sculptures and other artifacts, makes it evident that they are not the work of a single cultural occupation, and that prolonged periods must have been involved. In other words, it is clear that we cannot speak of one and only one San Agustín culture but must think in terms of a long sequence of different cultural phases, which in part evolved one from the other and in part represent successive occupations. The question that then arises is concerned with the age of the habitation sites and monuments and the chronological order in which they appeared.

The archaeologist's principal method of establishing the succession of different cultural phases has almost always been the detailed analysis of pottery remains. By excavating the discarded fragments of ceramic vessels, we can observe the subtle changes in technology, shape, and decoration that indicate a development in time and that serve to establish correlations between various sites. Lithic assemblages, consisting of discarded stone tools used for different purposes, can be employed in the same manner; bits of personal ornaments often appear as well, including scraps of metal or perhaps remains of food plants. There may be ash lenses from ancient hearths, living floors buried under the débris of later occupations, or post holes of wooden structures—in short, innumerable details that, when excavated stratigraphically, allow the archaeologist to reconstruct many aspects of the way of life of ancient peoples and to trace the slow development of settlements, land use, technological advance, trade, social organization, and religious practices. In a similar manner, the pottery associated with tombs can be seriated and a chronological sequence of burials established that can then be correlated with the sequence of ceramic types found in stratified midden or habitation sites.

Little of this kind of systematic research has been carried out thus far at San Agustín. This, as we have mentioned before, is mainly because of the emphasis most archaeologists have placed on the stone carvings—which are, of course, much more spectacular than the humble sherds or scrapers found in a refuse heap. The problem of chronology and development phases, with their exact cultural context, has thus remained largely in the background, and little is known about the continuity of cultural periods or the succession of different cultural traditions. Some recent researches, however, have produced results that make it possible to establish, at least in part, certain major periods of development, and I shall trace their outline here as far as the available evidence allows.

On the Mesitas site, at the Alto de los Idolos, El Tablón, Ciénaga Chica, and several other spots, great accumulations of occupational débris exist, large midden sites consisting of many layers of potsherds and lithic tools, occasionally reaching a depth of several meters. These accumulations are located both on level spots that have been occupied by habitations and on the slopes surrounding hilltops on which stood houses or villages whose inhabitants discarded broken vessels, stone tools, and kitchen refuse by throwing them down the slopes. Bits of charcoal, ash lenses, carbonized corn cobs, necklace beads, and a multitude of other small objects are contained in these middens. From the stratigraphic excavation of some of these refuse deposits, and from comparisons with other sites, it is possible to reconstruct the history of human occupation in certain sectors of the San Agustín region and to date some of its periods by the radiocarbon method.[1]

81　Mesita B. Anthropomorphic vessel found in burial site.

82   Isnos Period. Double-spouted vessel.

From these researches it appears that during the last centuries before the birth of Christ several localities, such as Las Mesitas, Alto de los Idolos, the slopes of the Cerro de la Horqueta, and the region of the Alto de las Piedras, were occupied by sedentary farmers whose remains mark the so-called Horqueta Period. These peoples, who seem to have lived in scattered houses on both sides of the Magdalena ravine, apparently did not construct major earthworks, nor did they attempt to level large extensions for habitation sites, but, rather, they occupied small living areas, often on sloping terrain. The farming and sedentary character of this occupation is indicated by fairly dense refuse containing grinding stones and many coarse scraping tools, accompanied by a large quantity of ceramic remains. The pottery of this period consists of several different types, among which vessels with a sharp peripheric angle are quite characteristic. These brown (or blackish) well-polished pots are frequently decorated with rectilinear incised motifs—other modes of decoration, such as paint or plastic ornaments, being generally absent (Plate 83). Some open bowls are adorned on the inside with a red slip, but otherwise the pottery is unpainted. The round-bottomed, rather heavy vessels, devoid of handles or spouts, are nevertheless competently made, and the range of forms and decorative designs clearly implies a long previous tradition. We have no absolute dates for this period, but from the available stratigraphic evidence we know that its remains consistently underlie those of other periods that have been dated by the radiocarbon method. On the other hand, from stylistic comparisons of the pottery we can deduce that the Horqueta Period is not too far removed in time from later developments.

During the early years of the first century A.D. a new development appeared with the Primavera Period.[2] The pottery and stone implements

83   Horqueta Period. Incised bowl.

84   Alto de Lavapatas. Carved head.

of this era are clearly derived from the preceding one, although typologically they form a new and distinct unit. The people of the Primavera
Period also occupied sites on both banks of the Magdalena River but
lived on hilltops, and were not as widely scattered as those of the Horqueta Period. The Primavera Period was followed in the latter part of
the first century A.D. by the Isnos Period, which represents a major change
in the cultural development of the entire region. There is little evidence
that this period was an outgrowth of the previous culture; it seems instead
that the entire San Agustín area was settled at that time by outside groups
who replaced, or partly assimilated, the culture of the former inhabitants.
There appears to have been during the Isnos Period a notable increase
in population density. Not only were the sites above mentioned reoccu-
pied but many others as well. Habitation sites were located on hilltops,
and all refuse was thrown down the slopes, on which eventually thick
layers of débris were formed (Plate 19). Occasionally these midden
accumulations were leveled artificially, probably to provide space for
more houses, and at other spots the refuse was used to fill in depressions
for the same purpose. In the vicinity of sites of this period large earthworks exist in the form of embankments, ridges, or flat expanses, and it
seems that this building and engineering activity was an outstanding
feature of the Isnos Period.[3]

Pottery remains are far more elaborate than those of the previous inhabitants. Ceramics of the Isnos Period are characterized by double-spouted vessels, bowls and dishes with negative painting, and a very typical light gray ware of a very hard consistency. Incised decoration is almost absent, and there is an emphasis on color, on bright shiny surfaces covered with a red slip or paint. Small clay figurines were manufactured, and occasionally a vessel was shaped in the form of a human head (Plate 85). Evidence of metallurgy is provided by droplets of molten gold and small bits of gold ornaments made from wire or plate. The Isnos Period lasted for several centuries, but we do not know its terminal date; the latest carbon date is A.D. 330, but there is evidence that these developments continued for a considerable time thereafter. Typologically, the ceramics of this period can be subdivided into several successive phases that provide proof of an uninterrupted internal development.

After the Isnos Period there follows a chronological hiatus. No stratified sites have been found so far to fill this wide gap, and we have only a number of undated surface collections of sherd materials that are probably representative of several periods, the detailed succession of which is not yet known. It is only in the second millennium A.D. that we again find datable strata. By 1410 the San Agustín region was occupied by a different people, who continued to live in this area until historic times, at least until 1640.[4] This occupation represented the Sombrerillos Period, spanning several centuries, during which most hills and slopes of the valley were settled by farming communities living in small clusters of circular houses built upon the level sites of the preceding inhabitants. The people of the Sombrerillos Period again represent a high population density, their remains being found all over the valley. The pottery made at that time is entirely different from that of other periods and consists of rather coarse reddish vessels. Characteristic shapes and decorative traits include tripods with solid conical supports,[5] corrugated vessels in which the coils of the structure are not smoothed on the surface but are used as a decorative device, straight-line incisions forming geometric patterns, and small cups decorated with a triangular design painted in black upon a red background. Although grinding stones are frequent and suggest maize cultivation, the extraordinary abundance of percussion-flaked scrapers may be indicative of a strong dependence upon root crops.

Two examples serve to illustrate this succession. On the western edge of the Mesitas plateau the sequence is as follows: originally the terrain was sloping almost forty-five degrees toward the depression covered at present by the so-called Grove of Statues. Early in the first century A.D. and for some time thereafter, a thick layer of occupational refuse accumulated, thrown down the slope by the inhabitants of a fairly large village located a short distance to the east, which represents the Isnos Period. This midden accumulation, which reaches a depth of almost two meters (six feet, seven inches), has been dated by radiocarbon from between A.D. 40 and 110. Some time after this date a large artificial fill was spread on top of the remains of the Isnos Period, burying them under a thick layer of soil, sometimes reaching three meters (nine feet, ten inches) in

85 Isnos Period. Double-spouted vessel.

depth. This fill, which consists of earth scraped together from the surface of some neighboring areas, contains sherds of two different ceramic complexes; many belong to the Isnos Period, but others are representative of the Bosque Period, whose exact time position is not known. The fill undoubtedly marks a period when major earthworks were carried out on the Mesitas site, but it was not built up to a horizontal level, its surface continuing to slope toward the west. On top of this fill lies another midden deposit about half a meter (one foot, eight inches) in depth, which consists of refuse belonging to the Sombrerillos Period and represents a late occupation.

86 (left)   Ullumbe.
Relief-carved boulder.

87   Alto de Lavaderos.
Statue with elongated
features.

88–90   La Chaquira. Relief-carved
boulders.

On the Alto de los Idolos the stratification is different. A five-meter-deep (sixteen feet, five inches) midden is stratified in the following manner: the oldest cultural layer consists of a thick deposit from the Primavera Period, at the bottom of which there are a few Horqueta sherds; the middle strata of this deposit are dated at A.D. 20. The top of the deposit was later leveled artificially, and a fill follows containing some Primavera sherds. However, the filling-in was accomplished in two successive steps, the first having a terminal date of A.D. 140. A thick layer of Isnos Period materials follows, dated in its middle at A.D. 330. After the Isnos Period this site was not occupied again.

From all stratigraphic data available so far, it seems that it was during the Isnos Period that notable engineering activity emerged, at least as far as major earthworks are concerned. This, however, does not imply

that stone constructions were executed at that time. On the contrary, from several stratigraphic tests made at the base of the barrows of the Mesitas plateau it appears that these, together with the stone chambers they contain, were constructed after A.D. 425, this being the latest of several carbon dates obtained for the midden deposits that underlie the barrows.[6]

The oldest carbon date obtained thus far for the San Agustín area is 555 B.C., which corresponds to a trough-shaped wooden coffin discovered in a tomb on the Alto de Lavapatas.[7] Unfortunately, the pottery associations were not recorded and we do not know the nature of the tomb furniture, so this date tells us very little besides the fact that fairly complex tombs were already under construction in the sixth century B.C. Seen within the wider context of San Agustín prehistory and of similar

92   Sombrerillos Period. Painted bowl.

91   Lavapatas. Bedrock carving on wall of pool.

developments in other parts of America, this date certainly does not mark an initial phase of local culture but already corresponds to an advanced stage.

The time position of the many different burial types is very difficult to ascertain, because no systematic study has been made of the respective grave associations. Urn burials seem to be a late trait, and the stone-lined tombs in the barrows can be dated after the fifth century A.D., but it would be mere guesswork to try to place other burial types on a precise time scale. Our lack of information in this respect is especially regrettable because it does not allow us to date the introduction and development of metallurgy at San Agustín. This is a point that deserves a few additional remarks.

Given the extraordinary wealth of prehistoric goldwork in Colombia, it is rather astonishing that so little of it should have been found at San Agustín. Most gold objects discovered so far were unearthed at burial sites, mainly in cist graves but also in some shaft tombs, and consist of small personal ornaments—nose rings, necklace beads, pendants, and ear hoops—made of gold wire or thin plates. The techniques employed in the manufacture of these objects ranged from cold hammering to lost-wax casting, and it is possible that these ornaments were made by local goldsmiths, judging from the droplets, bits of wire, and other waste materials that have been found in some middens. A remarkable object—which, although found in the neighboring Tierradentro region some 120 kilometers (75 miles) away, belongs stylistically to San Agustín—is a golden mask representing a feline motif (Plate 12). The object measures 14.3 centimeters (5.63 inches) in width and 6.7 centimeters (2.64 inches) in height and shows a protruding snout and fangs, the head being crowned by an elaborate ornamental band. The similarity to many other statues is striking, and it is a pity that we cannot assign even an approximate date to this extraordinary object. There is evidence for goldwork during the Isnos Period, but probably its use and technology were introduced at a far earlier date.

One of the most difficult problems of San Agustín prehistory concerns the chronological position of the stone carvings. The obstacles are many. First, as I mentioned earlier, many statues have been moved recently from their original locations, so we do not know the exact context in which they were standing in prehistoric times. Second, even if a statue is still standing on its original spot, sherds or other artifacts may have been deposited there at different time periods and do not necessarily date the sculpture. The San Agustín Indians, in their efforts to level certain areas, often brought large masses of fill containing sherds and other refuse from different localities, so the associations of a statue or barrow are not contemporary with their erection but may well be much older or pertain to many different periods. Finally, it seems that the stylistic patterns of decorative detail shown on the stone sculptures were not transferred to pottery decoration or to clay figurines, so we cannot establish valid correlations with the stratified middens. The best opportunity to date the sculptures would be provided by the discovery and careful excavation of a site hitherto undisturbed by treasure-hunters, where specific associations such as relationships to tomb structure, house sites, middens, or other factors could be observed. But, without this information, all efforts to put the statues into a chronological framework must remain speculation.

It is probable that the sculptures of the archaic and naturalistic styles are among the oldest monuments, especially if we agree that many of them seem to be derived from carving of tree trunks. Because many of them have been found in the general region of the Mesitas site, one might suggest that some of the earliest sculptors worked there. The main bulk of the statues of the expressionistic style, judging from their wide distribution and apparent association with earthworks, may correspond to the Isnos Period—which, in view of its elaborate pottery developments, its nucleated villages, and its building and engineering activity, could have been the period of greatest productivity in stone carvings. But two points must be taken into account here: in the first place, the expressionistic style can almost certainly be subdivided into several smaller stylistic units that cover a considerable timespan; in the second place, the Isnos Period also seems to have extended over many centuries, containing a series of related but distinct pottery complexes. The tentative correlation between the statues of the expressionistic style and the Isnos Period therefore lacks precision and must be judged in terms of a wide range of both groups and remains. The increasing tendency towards abstraction may have been a relatively late phenomenon, as may be the emphasis on relief-carved slabs. But all this is, admittedly, mere guesswork. Until we know more about the chronological phases of settlements and daily life, we cannot state with any certainty to which particular time the different statues pertain.

93   Quebradillas. Statue with staff.

To put ancient San Agustín into the wider context of prehistoric developments, I shall trace a brief outline of Colombian prehistory as far as it is
known at present.[1]

As is obvious from the country's geographical position, the earliest
inhabitants had come through Panama; Colombia, then, was the first
South American territory they occupied on their long march toward
the south. These early hunters and gatherers were already living in the
Bogotá highlands by the year 10,000 B.C.[2] and had probably established
themselves also in the Magdalena Valley and followed its course. Some
lithic assemblages (coarse scraping tools not associated with pottery)
have been found on the river terraces of the upper Magdalena River and
suggest the existence of small roaming bands of food-collectors. Very
little is known about this Paleo-Indian Stage, which lasted for many
thousands of years. More precise information begins only in the late
fourth millennium B.C. with the advent of the Archaic and early Formative stages. A number of large shell mounds discovered on the Caribbean
Coast have yielded a fairly complete picture of this distinctive form of
ecological adaptation, and there are sufficient absolute dates to place these
developments on a time scale. The artifact typology includes pottery (the
earliest in the Americas) and stone and shell objects, complemented by
abundant food remains in the form of mollusk shells and animal bones.
Subsistence activities and the selective use of various microenvironments
can be observed on the basis of these remains, and some indications of
social life can be found in the general layout of the sites. Carbon dates,
ranging roughly from 3100 B.C. to 1000 B.C., give evidence of considerable time–depth. Although most of these cultural remains were found
within the matrix of shell mounds located in the vicinity of shorelines or
estuaries, there also exists an inland variant of encampments on river-
banks and lagoons, where shellfish-gathering was being replaced by
fresh-water fishing and reptile-hunting.

Around 1000 B.C. the first sedentary villages with a subsistence basis
of root crops appeared. The technoeconomic aspects had radically changed
by then: a wide variety of ceramic shapes, techniques, and decorative
elements made their appearance, together with an emphasis on larger
stone tools, many of them ground or even polished. The staple food was
then of vegetable origin, and only fishing continued to provide proteins,
while hunting and shellfish-gathering seem to have been abandoned.

During the first millennium B.C. or perhaps earlier, a new pattern of life developed on much of the lowlands. Permanent settlements were established at a distance from the coast, on the shores of inland lagoons, near the lower stretches of the rivers where abundant reptiles and the yearly run of fish, combined with root-cropping, provided permanent food resources. Again there was a jump in the diversity and combination of artifact assemblages, and pottery was becoming a more and more sensitive guide to changes in time and space.

With the advent of intensified seed agriculture, traceable in the large grinding stones, mullers, pestles, and new pottery shapes, this pattern of life changed again. We now observe a tendency toward decentralization that was manifested in the abandonment of the riverine and lacustrine environment and the establishment of small scattered groups of houses on hill slopes and in mountainfolds. Maize was becoming the staple food that made sedentary life possible on a rugged terrain, away from the main rivers. Bedrock mortars, anthropomorphic pottery, large storage vessels for liquids, and other ceramic traits were characteristic, and there were large quantities of stone celts for clearing the land. Copper and gold, sometimes *tumbaga*, an alloy of gold with copper, appeared, and trade was maintained between the coast and inland settlements. With intensive maize farming an entirely new range of local adaptations became possible; this led inevitably in this diversified environment of the interior provinces to isolation in mountainfolds, to regionalism in small valleys, and to the development of a mosaic of local traditions.

The archaeological evidence seems to indicate that in certain regions of the country some maize-farming communities were more successful than others.[3] The depth of the midden deposits, the abundance of grinding stones, and the general advance of the technotypological level give proof of a stable economic basis, a situation that was not achieved equally or simultaneously in all regions. This efficiency was probably reached not only through intensive maize farming but also through extensive trade relations. These communities also appear to have reached a degree of political cohesion and ceremonialism that went beyond the confines of a small region circumscribed by a valley or river basin. The archaeological record shows that there was a certain unity in settlement patterns and in subsistence activities, in pottery styles and decorative elements, and also in religious symbolism as manifested in ceremonial sites and associated objects.

This then represents a new development characterized by certain material remains. Architectural features such as stone foundations, small retention walls, terraces, leveled platforms, and other earthworks are found in these regions, together with modeled pottery, shaft graves, burial urns, and metal work. If we interpret the architectural and engineering features as public works and observe the differential burial associations and luxury goods, we can conclude that these were stratified societies that were emerging now from the simple farming level. The regions that fall into this cultural category are the Sinú and San Jorge valleys, the foothills of the Sierra Nevada of Santa Marta, certain parts of the lower Magdalena Valley, some of the intermontane valleys of the

94 Alto de Lavapatas. Slab with pecked grooves outlining face.

Central Cordillera, the Bogotá highlands, and the Andean core-land of the Colombian Massif. It is there where the so-called Sub-Andean culture pattern was beginning to develop, starting during the last centuries B.C. and evolving later on into the chiefdoms that lasted into the sixteenth century.

In a few regions, all of them of limited geographical extension, this development reached a climax. In the Sierra Nevada appeared an architectural complex with nucleated villages built on stone foundations and interconnected by a network of stone-paved roads. Agricultural terraces are found on the slopes, and irrigation farming was practiced on the neighboring arid plains. Pottery, metallurgy, and fine lapidary arts were highly developed, and the Tairona culture emerges as perhaps the highest cultural achievement of the Colombian aborigines. In the Bogotá

95   Mesita B, northwest slope. Relief-carved boulder.

highlands the Chibcha appeared, a culture represented by a large and scattered rural population practicing intensive farming and reaching a notable development in pottery, metallurgy, small stone carvings, and trade. In both the Sierra Nevada and the Bogotá highlands, groups of chiefdoms had united and small states were in the process of formation when the Spanish conquest put an end to these developments.[4]

The evidence for these different stages, from Paleo-Indian hunters and gatherers to chiefdoms and village federations, is of course far from complete, but it is sufficiently well defined at a large number of sites to allow us to trace the main lines of development. Although some regions remain to be explored and many aspects of the principal stages are still inadequately known, the over-all scheme presented above seems to be reasonably well founded.

In this slow development of prehistoric cultures in Colombia, external influences played a major part. To an old common substratum underlying all aboriginal cultures from Mexico to Chile, later successive migrations and contacts added new elements. Mesoamerica's greatest gift to South America was maize, but there were also many other aspects of culture that traveled south and stimulated local developments here and there. Nor were these contacts restricted to a north-to-south influx: Many trends were also traveling northward in different time periods. Mesoamerican contacts with the central Andes go back at least to 1500 B.C. and surely did not bypass Colombia without having left some traces, and there is clear evidence for strong Mesoamerican influences on the southern Pacific Coast of Colombia at about 500 B.C. Some of these coastal developments spread inward to the inter-Andean valleys, and it also seems that certain trends were diffused along the inland mountain ranges.

It was within this general framework that San Agustín developed, not as a specialized "ceremonial center" but as a cluster of simple farming communities that went through essentially the same stages of growth, from a former riverine environment to root-cropping, and from root-cropping to maize-farming. At some time when subsistence resources had reached a level of efficiency and stability that led to the establishment of nucleated village life, ceremonialism began to take form, developing in channels conditioned by local needs and precedents—but never in isolation: from one stage of development to the next, from one period to the other, there always existed contacts with the wider scene, by war or migration, trade or marriage, or simply the spread of ideas.

We know nothing yet of the early Formative beginnings in the San Agustín area, but certain stray finds of pottery—sherds decorated with rocker-stamped designs or with broad-shallow line incisions—suggest a ceramic tradition that goes back in time to the early centuries of the first millennium B.C., perhaps even farther. A similar date might be suggested for the first material manifestations of the feline motif, which in Mesoamerica and the Central Andes appears on an even earlier time level. On this basis, it seems, the earliest sedentary villages developed; after the introduction of intensive maize-growing,[5] these grew into one of the many inter-Andean communities, some of which developed into small chiefdoms.

96 and 97 Mesita B,
South Barrow. Slabs with
incised designs.

98 Alto de los Idolos.
Column with incised figure.

We must distinguish here among various levels on which comparisons may be made. There is a very ancient level of widespread ideas, which many aboriginal peoples apparently held in common in Nuclear America, but which does not necessarily prove any active contact between these groups. Some of these underlying ideas would be concept of a supernatural Master of Animals, of the jaguar-monster, of human-head trophies, of the symbolic value of certain minerals (such as quartz, obsidian, jade, turquoise, or gold), or of color symbolism. These ideas were likely to find quite different stylistic expressions in various regions, which cannot be compared because the exterior forms they took were the results of specific environmental conditions. The important point is the verifiable extent of the idea, and not its divergences in detail. Among these primary ideas may also be counted the combination of jaguar-bird-fish-snake and, most probably, the imagery of dwarflike spirit-beings with phallic associations. On this level, then, San Agustín clearly belongs to the ideological sphere lying between the Olmec and Chavín, the two great centers where the jaguar-monster found its principal expression in stone sculpture. There are no clear stylistic relationships between these two cultures, nor between either of them and San Agustín, but it is unmistakable that all three share a common thematic core.

On another level we are dealing with diffusion, be it of secondary ideas or of artifact traditions. Such secondary ideas might be the *alter ego* motif, monolithic sarcophagi, or mounds with sepulchral chambers, which may have spread by migration, superimposing themselves upon

99 Alto de los Idolos. Table-shaped "altar."

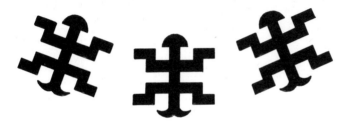

Fig. 17   Gold pendants from grave, El Batán.

the old common substratum. From the existing evidence, however, it would be very difficult indeed to use these traits to establish links between one culture and another, and still more difficult to tell in which direction they were diffused. There were certain similarities between the early pottery complexes of Mexico and Peru, approximately between 1000 B.C. and 600 B.C., but so far San Agustín has not yielded any evidence for close and well-defined relationships with this horizon, although it may well be present and may someday be found.

Beyond these possible points of comparison are others. With reference to pottery developments, the oldest complex identified so far (represented by the Horqueta Period) shows certain similarities with pottery from the Andean highlands of southern Colombia and northern Ecuador, suggesting migrations or at least mutual influences along the Andean spine during the last centuries B.C. During the first half of the first millennium A.D. this southern influence tended to disappear and with the advent of the Isnos Period was replaced by marked similarities with Cauca Valley pottery. Double-spouted vessels, negative paint, and a general emphasis on painted decoration or brightly slipped surfaces point to relationships with the central and western provinces and the so-called Quimbaya and Calima areas. These regions, where there existed in the early sixteenth century some of the more advanced chiefdoms, furnishes many other parallels, but unfortunately, as is the case with the Andean region, there is no chronological framework yet for these parts of the country, and all comparisons are therefore based on stylistic similarities alone. For example, the sculptured head ornament of a guardian statue at Mesita A can be compared with certain gold objects from the Central Cordillera, the same as the H-shaped gold plaques found in a shaft tomb at San Agustín that also yielded several biomorphic gold pendants belonging to the so-called Tolima style (Figure 17). Nose rings the shape of that worn by the statue of El Tablón (Plate 79) are fairly frequent in the goldwork of the inter-Andean regions. The feline motif is quite common in the gold originating from the Calima region, farther to the west, especially in certain masklike ornaments on which human features are combined with the muzzle and fangs of a snarling jaguar. Some abstract geometric elements are also comparable. But again, we are hampered by the lack of a precise time scale, stratigraphic excavations, and clear-cut cultural sequences.

Many attempts have been made to compare the statues of San Agustín with those of other centers of aboriginal stone carving and to link them to certain developments to the north and south of Colombia. As far as Mesoamerica is concerned, except for the underlying ideological base, no formal relationships can be said to exist. Only in Central America, especially in Nicaragua, do we occasionally find statues with the blocklike quality so characteristic of South American carvings, which points to a tradition of wooden sculptures on tree trunks. Most Costa Rican and Panamanian stone sculpture shows voids and internal spaces, often freeing the limbs from the body, quite unlike any South American sculptures. External relationships point then rather to the Central Andes, and so it seems that San Agustín stands both sculpturally and stylistically between Chavín and Tiahuanaco, being neither as curvilinear and asymmetrical as the former nor as rectilinear and balanced as the latter. But this position involves a long time span, and too little is known about the chronology of sculptural developments in the Andean highlands to warrant more precise correlations.

100   Alto de los Idolos. Carved slab.

San Agustín is not the only place in Colombia where prehistoric stone sculptures have been found, although in no other region are they as numerous and elaborate. In neighboring Tierradentro there exist several statues that, in many aspects, are similar to San Agustín, although they represent human beings and are considerably less stylized. Toward the Cauca Valley, in the region of Moscopán, one of several statues is a quite realistic portrait of a man, but it is done in the San Agustín style. In the southern highlands small, coarse sculptures are found, similar to the peg-shaped statues of San Agustín; even near the headwaters of the Caquetá River stone sculptures have been found. Near Colombia, a small village at the foot of the Sumapaz Massif, close to the mountain pass toward the Orinoco drainage, fairly large and crude statues have been discovered, and in the highlands north of Bogotá others exist. In the north, in the foothills of the Sierra Nevada of Santa Marta, a few isolated stone carvings stand. None of these sculptures have been correlated with a wider cultural context of domestic or ceremonial remains, so their chronological position is uncertain. Only some of the statues

from Tierradentro and perhaps Moscopán can be said to belong essentially to the sculptural tradition of San Agustín, and those of the other regions mentioned above may well have been local developments not connected in any significant way with the sculptor's art of San Agustín.

But these problems of chronology and external relationships will eventually be solved. From the available evidence we can deduce that San Agustín is not an isolated phenomenon but that its ancient roots lie embedded in the wide common substratum extending from Mexico to Bolivia, the core-land of aboriginal culture in the Americas. On this basis, San Agustín developed much like other communities, except for its extraordinary stone carvings. In these sculptures the ancient Indians of the Colombian Massif created for themselves a lasting monument that no one who has once beheld it is likely to forget.

101 Alto de Lavapatas. Carved slab.

Selected Bibliography

CALDAS, FRANCISCO JOSÉ DE. "Estado de la Geografía del Virreinato de Santa Fé de Bogotá, con relacion a la economía y el comercio," in *Semanario del Nuevo Reino de Granada*. Bogotá: n.p., 1942.

CODAZZI, AGUSTÍN. "Ruinas de San Agustín," in Felipe Pérez, ed., *Geografía física i política de los Estados Unidos de Colombia* 2 (Bogotá, 1863): 76–106.

CUERVO MÁRQUEZ, CARLOS. *Estudios arqueológicos y etnográficos americanos: Prehistoria y viajes americanos*. Madrid, 1920.

DUQUE GÓMEZ, LUÍS. "Los últimos hallazgos arqueológicos de San Agustín," *Revista del Instituto Etnológico Nacional* 2 (Bogotá, 1946): 5–41.
———. *San Agustín: Reseña Arqueológica*. Bogotá: Instituto Colombiano de Antropología, 1963.
———. *Exploraciones arqueológicas en San Agustín*, Bogotá: Instituto Colombiano de Antropología, 1964.

FRIEDE, JUAN. *Los Andakí 1538–1947: Historia de la aculturación de una tribu selvática*. Mexico City: Fondo de Cultura Económica, 1953.

GUHL, ERNESTO. "El Macizo Colombiano: Informe preliminar sobre un ensayo etnográfico," *Boletín de Arqueología* 1, No. 3 (Bogotá, 1945): 257–65.

GUTIERREZ DE ALBA, JOSÉ MARÍA. "Noticia de un monumento prehistórico: las estatuas del valle de San Agustín," *Boletín de la Sociedad Geográfica* 27 (Madrid, 1889): 363–83.

HERNÁNDEZ DE ALBA, GREGORIO. *Guía arqueológica de San Agustín o del Macizo Central de los Andes*. Bogotá: n.p., 1943.
———. "The Archaeology of San Agustín and Tierradentro, Colombia," *Handbook of South American Indians* 2, Bureau of American Ethnology Bulletin 143 (Washington, D.C., 1946): 851–59.

KUBLER, GEORGE. *The Art and Architecture of Ancient America*, The Pelican History of Art 84. Harmondsworth, England: Penguin, 1962.

LUNARDI, FEDERICO. *El Macizo Colombiano en la Prehistoria de Sur América*. Río de Janeiro, 1934.

NACHTIGALL, HORST. *Die Amerikanischen Megalithkulturen: Vorstudien zu einer Untersuchung*. Berlin: Dietrich Reimer-Verlag, 1958.
———. "Zur Chronologie der Tierradentro—und San Agustín-Kultur," *Zeitschrift für Ethnologie* 89, No. 1 (Brunswick, 1964): 78–81.

PÉREZ DE BARRADAS, JOSÉ. "Máscara de oro de Inzá," *Revista de las Indias*, No. 1 (Bogotá, 1937), pp. 3–7.
———. "Estudio Antropológico de los primeros dos cráneos humanos de la cultura de San Agustín," *Revista de la Academia de Ciencias Exactas, Físicas y Naturales* 2, No. 7 (Bogotá, 1938): 371–76.
———. *Arqueología Agustiniana*. Bogotá: Ministerio de Educación Nacional, 1943.

PREUSS, KONRAD THEODOR. "Bericht über meine archäologischen und ethnologischen Forschungsreisen in Kolumbien," *Zeitschrift für Ethnologie* 52 (Berlin, 1922): 89–128.
———. "Die Darstellung des Zweiten Ich unter den Indianern Amerikas," *In Memoriam Karl Weule*. Leipzig: n.p., 1929.
———. *Monumentale vorgeschichtliche Kunst, Ausgrabungen im Quellgebiet des Magdalena in Kolumbien, 1913-1914*. Göttingen: Vandenhoeck & Ruprecht, 1929.

REICHEL-DOLMATOFF, GERARDO. *Colombia: Ancient Peoples and Places*. London: Thames & Hudson; New York: Praeger Publishers, 1965.

RIVERO, EDUARDO MARINAO DE, and JOHANN JAKOB VON TSCHUDI. *Antigüedades Peruanas* (Text and Atlas). Vienna, 1851.

SCHOTTELIUS, JUSTUS WOLFRAM. "Bosquejo comparativo entre las deidades representadas por las estatuas de San Agustín, y las de Mexico y las de los Chibchas," *Boletín de la Sociedad Geográfica de Colombia* 6, Nos. 2–3 (Bogotá, 1939): 169–86.

STÖPEL, KARL THEODOR. *Südamerikanische Prähistorische Tempel und Gottheiten*. Frankfurt, 1912.
———. "Archaeological discovery in Ecuador and Southern Colombia during 1911 and the ancient stone monuments of San Agustín," *Proceedings of the XVIII International Congress of Americanists*, London, 1912.

UHLE, MAX. "Herkunft und Alter der frühgeschichtlichen Denkmäler von San Agustín in Colombien," *Ibero-Amerikanisches Archiv* 11 (Berhu, 1937–38): 327–32.

WALDE-WALDEGG, HERMANN VON. "Preliminary Report on the Expedition to San Agustín (Colombia)," *Anthropological Series of the Boston College* 2, No. 7, (Boston, 1937): 5–54.

Wavrin, Marquis de. "Apport aux connaissances de la civilisation dite de San Agustín et à l'archéologie du sud de la Colombie," *Bulletin de la Société des Américanistes de Belgique*, No. 21 (Brussels, 1936), pp. 107–34.

Ziegert, Helmut. "Zur Chronologie der Tierradentro—und San Augustin-Kultur, (Kolumbien), *Zeitshrift für Ethnologie* 87 (Brunswick, 1962): 51–55.
———. "Zur Chronologie der Tierradentro—und San Agustín-Kultur," *Zeitschrift für Ethnologie* 91 (Brunswick, 1966): 114–15.

Table of Radio-Carbon Dates from San Agustín

SITE AND ASSOCIATIONS	PERIOD	LAB. NO.	DIG	B.P. DATE	DATE
Mesitas, NE end of plateau, middle layer of midden	Sombrerillos	I–2310	GRD	320±90	A.D. 1630
Mesitas, NE end of plateau, bottom layer of midden	Sombrerillos	I–2309	GRD	540±110	A.D. 1410
Potrero de Lavapatas, charcoal from house site		GRN–3447	GRD	770±120	A.D. 1180
Mesita B, NW Barrow, burial beneath mound		Isotopes	LDG	1525±150	A.D. 420
Alto de los Idolos midden	Late Isnos	I–2316	GRD	1620±100	A.D. 330
Mesita B, NW Barrow, midden beneath mound		Isotopes	LDG	1800±100	A.D. 150
Alto de los Idolos midden	Late Isnos	I–2317	GRD	1810±100	A.D. 140
Mesitas, W edge, midden	Early Isnos	I–2312	GRD	1840±110	A.D. 110
Mesitas, W edge, midden	Early Isnos	I–2314	GRD	1850±100	A.D. 100
Mesitas, W edge, midden	Early Isnos	I–2313	GRD	1900±140	A.D. 50
Mesitas, W edge, midden	Early Isnos	I–2315	GRD	1910±110	A.D. 40
Alto de los Idolos, midden	Primavera	I–2318	GRD	1930±120	A.D. 20
Mesita B, NW Barrow, midden beneath mound		GRN–3643	LDG	1930±50	A.D. 20
Mesitas, W edge, midden		GRN–4205	LDG	1960±50	10 B.C.
Alto de Lavapatas, coffin		GRN–3016	JPB	2505±50	555 B.C.

Abbreviations: I = Isotopes Inc., GRN = Gröningen, GRD = G. Reichel-Dolmatoff, LDG = L. Duque Gómez, JPB = J. Pérez de Barradas.

Notes on the Text

Chapter I

1 For a good general introduction to Colombian geography, see *Atlas de Colombia* (Bogotá: Instituto Geográfico Agustín Codazzi, 1967). Other useful works of reference are Pablo Vila, *Nueva Geografía de Colombia* (Bogatá, 1945); *Atlas de Economía Colombiana* (Bogotá: Banco de la República, 1959–62).

2 On the geography of the Colombian Massif, see Joaquín Emilio Cardozo, "Monografía Geográfica sobre el Macizo de los Andes Colombianos o Nudo Andino, y sobre el Alto Caquetá," *Boletín de la Sociedad Geográfica* de Colombia 5, No. 2 (Bogotá, 1938): 157–73; Ernesto Guhl, "El Macizo Colombiano," *Boletín de Arqueología* 5 (Bogotá, 1945): 435–43; Justo Ramón, *Las fuentes de los ríos Magdalena y Caquetá* (Bogotá, 1947).

3 The village is located at Greenwich 1° 52′ 54″ N, 76° 15′ 47″ W.

Chapter II

1 Clements R. Markham, *The Travels of Pedro Cieza de León* (New York: Burt Franklin, n.d.).

2 On the Andakí, see Juan Friede, *Los Andakí* (Mexico City: Fondo de Cultura Económica, 1953).

3 For historical data on the San Agustín region, see Luís Duque Gómez, *Exploraciones Arqueólogicas en San Agustín* (Bogotá, 1964).

4 Fray Juan de Santa Gertrudis, *Maravillas de la Naturaleza*, 2 vols. (Bogotá, 1956).

5 At the time of Friar Juan, amethysts were still of great value and were used in bishops' rings. They lost much of their value after the discovery of the rich deposits of Minas Germais, Brazil, in the early nineteenth century.

6 Francisco José de Caldas, "Estado de la Geografía del Virreinato de Santa Fé de Bogotá, con relación a la economía y el comercio," in *Semanario del Nuevo Reino de Granada* (Bogotá, n.p., 1942).

7 Eduardo Mariano de Rivero and Johann Jakob von Tschudi, *Antigüedades Peruanas* (text and atlas) (Vienna, 1851).

8 Agustín Codazzi, "Ruines de San Agustín," in Felipe Pérez, *Jeografía fisica y política de los Estados Unidos de Colombia* 2 (Bogotá, 1863): 76–106.

9 Carlos Cuervo Márquez, *Prehistoria y Viajes: Estudios arqueológicos y etnográficos* (Madrid, 1920).

10 Karl Theodor Stöpel, *Südamerikanische Prähistorische Tempel und Gottheiten* (Frankfurt, 1912).

11 Karl Theodor Stöpel, "Archaeological Discovery in Ecuador and Southern Colombia during 1911 and the Ancient Stone Monuments of San Agustín," *Proceedings of the XVIII International Congress of Americanists* (London, 1912).

12 Konrad Theodor Preuss, "Bericht über meine archäeologischen und ethnologischen Forschungsreisen in Kolumbien," *Zeitschrift für Ethnologie* 52 (Berlin, 1922): 89–128; *id.*, "Die Darstellung des Zweiten Ich unter den Indianern Amerikas," in *In Memoriam Karl Weule* (Leipzig, 1929); and *id.*, *Monumentale vorgeschichtliche Kunst, Ausgrabungen im Quellgebiet des Magdalena in Kolumbien, 1913–1914*, 2 vols. (Göttingen, 1929).

13 José Pérez de Barradas, *Arqueología Agustiniana* (Bogotá, 1943).

14 Luís Duque Gómez, *Exploraciones arqueológicas en San Agustín* (Bogotá: Instituto Colombiano de Antropología, 1964).

Chapter III

1 No aerial photographs of the San Agustín region are available, and the few existing maps are of very poor quality.

2 With the exception of the Mesitas plateau, there exist no detailed site surveys.

3 Although Colombia has excellent antiquity laws it is extremely difficult to enforce them, and treasure-hunters continue to destroy many important sites. During recent years the illegal trade of prehistoric art objects has reached alarming proportions.

4 In spite of its gigantic size Preuss, who explored this site in detail, did not find it. This gives us a measure of the density of the forest some fifty years ago.

Chapter IV

1 The aspect that some of the barrows of the Mesitas site offer at present is rather misleading. They were reconstructed in recent years according to Pérez de Barradas's hypothesis, which, although interesting, lacks supporting evidence.

2 This information is of interest in view of what will be said of similar stone carvings in Chapter VI.

3 Besides, it has been reconstructed recently.

4 Luís Duque Gómez, "Los últimos hallazgos arqueológicos de San

Agustín," *Revista del Instituto Etnológico Nacional* 2 (Bogotá, 1946): 5–41, expresses the belief that the statue represents a pregnant woman and that most of the associated skeletons are female.

5 This grave is located immediately in front of the gigantic statue illustrated in Plate 69.

6 Unfortunately, the skeletal remains discovered in these burials have not been studied by physical anthropologists. The only study published so far is José Pérez de Barradas, "Estudio Antropológico de los primeros dos cráneos humanos de la cultura de San Agustín," *Revista de la Academia de Ciencias Exactas, Físicas y Naturales* 2, No. 7 (Bogotá, 1938): 371–76, and refers to two skulls.

Chapter V

1 In analyzing the stone carvings, I have mainly followed the outline of L. R. Rogers, *Sculpture* (London: Oxford University Press, 1969).

2 The crouching female statue from Quinchana (Figure 11) is the only exception.

3 Hundreds of these stone mauls have been found near the East Barrow of Mesita A. See Duque Gómez, *Exploraciones arqueológicas, supra,* Ch. II, note 14, Plate xxxiv.

4 This might suggest their use as piers.

5 The group shown standing on the North Barrow of Mesita B (Plate 24) has been assembled there as a tourist attraction. The statues originally came from different localities.

6 George Kubler, *The Art and Architecture of Ancient America,* The Pelican History of Art 84 (Harmondsworth, England: Penguin, 1962), has tried to combine eye and nose shapes to establish a typology.

7 Strangely enough, the same design is used to represent the nose of the statue in Plate 67.

Chapter VI

1 Preuss, *Monumentale vorgeschichtliche Kunst (supra,* Ch. II, note 12), Vol. I, Plate 8: 3, 4; Plate 9: 1, 2.

2 Jaguar representations of the Amazon basin often show this coiled or curled tail end. See Henry S. Wassén, "Om några indianska droger och speciellt om snus samt tillbehör," *Arstryck 1963–1966* (Göteborg: Etnografiska Museet, 1967), pp. 97–140; and *id.,* "Anthropological Survey of the Use of South American Snuffs," in Daniel H. Efron, ed., *Ethnopharmacologic Search for Psychoactive Drugs* (Washington, D.C.: U.S. Department of Health, Education, and Welfare, 1967), pp. 233, 289.

3 In the Central Andes, the main archaeological areas where the jaguar motif is common are Chavín, Paracas, Moche, Nazca, and Tiahuanaco. In Mesoamerica the motif spreads from the Olmec area of Veracruz over much of Mexico and Guatemala.

4 Heinz Walter, *Der Jaguar in der Vorstellungswelt der Südamerikanischen Indianer* (doctoral dissertation, University of Hamburg, 1956).

5 Among the best sources on the Olmecs are Elizabeth P. Benson, ed., *Dumbarton Oaks Conference on the Olmec* (Washington, 1968); Ignacio Bernal, *The Olmec World* (Berkeley and Los Angeles: University of California Press, 1969); Michael D. Coe, *The Jaguar's Children: Pre-Classic Central Mexico* (New York: The Museum of Primitive Art, 1965); and *id.*, *America's First Civilization: Discovering the Olmec* (New York: The Smithsonian Library, 1968).

6 Matthew W. Stirling, "Stone Monuments of Río Chiquito, Veracruz, Mexico," *Bureau of American Ethnology*, Bulletin 157, *Anthropological Paper No. 43* (Washington, 1955).

7 It seems that the oldest feline representations in Colombia occur at the Momil site, a village midden of the Formative Stage on the Caribbean Coast. See G. Reichel-Dolmatoff and A. Reichel-Dolmatoff, "Momil: Excavaciones en el río Sinú," *Revista Colombiana de Antropología* 5 (Bogotá, 1956): 111–222.

8 G. Reichel-Dolmatoff, *Colombia: Ancient Peoples and Places* (London: Thames and Hudson, 1965).

9 Some sculptures were destroyed by over-zealous missionaries.

10 Markham, *Travels of Pedro Cieza de León, supra*, Ch. II, note 1, p. 59.

11 *Ibid.*, p. 48.

12 Pedro de Aguado, *Recopilación Historical* 1 (Bogotá, 1956): 598.

13 G. Reichel-Dolmatoff, *Los Kogi: Una tribu de la Sierra Nevada de Santa Marta, Colombia*, 2 vols. (Bogotá, 1950–51).

14 G. Reichel-Dolmatoff, *Desana: Simbolismo de los Indios Tukano del Vaupés* (Bogotá: Universidad de los Andes, 1968).

15 Tierradentro is only 120 kilometers (75 miles) from San Agustín. Some of the major sources on the Páez Indians are Segundo Bernal Villa, "Aspectos de la Cultura Páez: Mitología y Cuentos de la parcialidad de Calderas, Tierradentro," *Revista Colombiana de Antropología* 1 (Bogotá, 1953): 279–309; *id.*, "Medicina y Magia entre los Páez," *Revista Colombiana de Antropología* 2 (Bogotá, 1954): 219–64; Horst Nachtigall, "Schamanismus bei den Páez Indianern," *Zeitschrift für Ethnologie* 78, No. 2 (Brunswick, 1955): 210–23; Jesús M. Otero, *Etnología Caucana* (Popayán, 1952).

16 Otero, *Etnología Caucana*, pp. 89–91.

17 Juan de Vadillo, "Carta del Lycenciado Xoan de Vadillo a su Magestad, dándole quenta de su vysita a la Gobernación de Cartagena, Cartagena, Octubre 15 de 1537," *Colección de documentos inéditos relatives al descubrimiento, conquista y colonización de las posesiones españolas en América y Oceanía*, vol. 41 (Madrid, 1884).

18 This concept of the Kogi has had archaeological confirmation, a jaguar skull having been found in the context of a ceremonial structure.

19 Reichel-Dolmatoff, *Desana*, p. 20.

20 *Ibid.*, p. 57.

21 Reichel-Dolmatoff, *Los Kogi*, Vol. 1, 267–68.

22 Michael D. Coe, *Mexico: Ancient Peoples and Places* (London: Thames and Hudson, 1962), p. 85.

23 Miguel Covarrubias, *Mexico South* (New York: Knopf, 1954), and *id.*, *Indian Art of Mexico and Central America* (New York: Knopf, 1957).

24 Covarrubias, *Mexico South*, pp. 98–99.

25 Reichel-Dolmatoff, *Desana*, *passim*.

26 *Ibid.*, p. 99.

27 *Ibid.*, pp. 99–100.

28 *Ibid.*, p. 57.

29 During certain ceremonial dances the Kogi Indians sing: "We are sons of the jaguar; we are evil jaguars; we devour women."

30 See, among others, Richard Evans Schultes, "The Identity of Malpighiaceous Narcotics of South America," *Botanical Museum Leaflets, Harvard University* 18 (Cambridge, 1957): 1–56; *id.*, "Botanic Sources of New World Narcotics," *Psychedelic Review* 1 (1963): 145–66; *id.*, "The Botanical Origins of South American Snuffs," in Daniel H. Efron, ed., *Ethnopharmacological Search for Psychoactive Drugs* (Washington, D.C.: U.S. Department of Health, Education, and Welfare, 1967): 233–89; Wassén, "Anthropological Survey of Use of Snuffs" *supra*, note 2; Néstor Uscátegui M., "The Present Distribution of Narcotics and Stimulants Amongst the Indian Tribes of Colombia," *Botanical Museum Leaflets* 18, No. 6 (Cambridge: Harvard University Press, 1959): 273–304.

31 Pedro de Aguado, *Recopilacion Historical* 1.

32 Wassén, "Om några indianska," *supra*, note 2.

33 Joaquín Rocha, *Memorandum de Viaje: Regiones Amazónicas* (Bogotá, 1905), 43–45.

34 G. Reichel-Dolmatoff, "La cultura material de los indios Guahibo," *Revista del Instituto Etnológico Nacional* 1, No. 2 (Bogotá, 1944): 437–506.

35 Horst Nachtigall, *Tierradentro: Archäeologie und Ethnographic einer kulumbianischen Landschaft* (Zurich, 1955), p. 308.

36 Preuss, "Die Darstellung des Zweiten," *supra*, Ch. II, note 12; Otto Zerries, "Die Vorstellung vom Zweiten Ich und die Rolle der Harpye in der Kultur der Naturvölker Südamerikas," *Anthropos* 57 (Fribourg, 1962): 889–914. Eliade says: "This alter ego is one of the shaman's 'souls,' the 'soul in animal form,' or, more precisely, the 'life soul.' Shamans challenge one another in animal form, and if his alter ego is killed in the fight, the shaman very soon dies himself." Mircea Eliade, *Shamanism: Archaic Techniques of Ecstasy*, Bollingen Series 86 (New York, 1964).

37 Wassén, "Om några indianska."

38 Peter T. Furst, "The Olmec Were-Jaguar Motif in the Light of Ethnographic Reality," Elizabeth P. Benson, ed., *Dumbarton Oaks Conference on the Olmec* (Washington, 1968) pp. 143–78. This excellent paper is of special interest in our discussion.

39 Reichel-Dolmatoff, *Los Kogi* 1: 181.

40 *Ibid.*, 1: 204.

41 *Ibid.*, 1: 268–69.

42 Reichel-Dolmatoff, *Desana*, pp. 65, 76.

43 Markham, *Travels of Pedro Cieza de Leon*.

Chapter VII

1 The following chronological considerations are mainly based upon the author's own stratigraphic excavations.
2 The names of the different periods are derived from those of the type-sites where the respective period was identified.
3 The construction of large earthworks suggest a strong political organization.
4 There is no evidence that this period corresponds to the historic Andakí.
5 According to Duque Gómez, *Exploraciones arqueológicas en San Agustín, supra,* Ch. II, note 14, tripod vessels are considerably older at San Agustín, but no evidence has been found to support this affirmation.
6 *Ibid.,* p. 456.
7 *Ibid.*

Chapter VIII

1 For a general outline of Colombian prehistory, see G. Reichel-Dolmatoff, *Colombia: Ancient Peoples and Places* (London: Thames and Hudson, 1965).
2 The El Abra site near Zipaquirá, some forty kilometers (twenty-six miles) north of Bogotá, is characterized by several small rock shelters, which contain midden refuse. The lithic assemblages consist mainly of percussion shaped scrapers; no projectile points have been found so far.
3 G. Reichel-Dolmatoff, "The Agricultural Basis of the Sub-Andean Chiefdoms of Colombia," in Johannes Wilbert, ed., *The Evolution of Horticultural Systems in Native South America: Causes and Consequences* (Caracas: Sociedad de Ciencias Naturales, 1961,) pp. 83–100.
4 The conquest of the Chibcha highlands began in 1538. For a recent historical account see Juan Friede, *La invasión del país de los Chibchas* (Bogotá, 1966).
5 The carbonized corn-cobs found at San Agustín are very small (about four centimeters long).

Plates

1 Upper Magdalena Valley.
2 Magdalena Ravine Seen from Chaquira Site.
3 Main Statue, Mesita A, West Barrow. Height: 2.04 meters (6 feet, 8¼ inches).
4 Detail of Guardian Statue, Mesita A, East Barrow.
5 Tomb at Mesitas Site, an 1825 drawing.
6 Two Statues from Mesitas, an 1825 drawing.
7 Statue from Mesita A, an 1853 watercolor. Height: 2.23 meters (7 feet, 3¾ inches).
8 Statue from Mesita A, an 1854 watercolor.
9 Cerro de la Horqueta.
10 Remains of Subterranean Chamber, Mesitas, South Barrow.
11 Large Triangular Face, Mesita B. Height: 2.26 meters (7 feet, 5 inches).
12 Gold Mask of Jaguar-Monster, Inza. Width: 14.3 centimeters (5.63 inches); height: 6.7 centimeters (2.64 inches). Collection Museo del Oro, Banco de la Republica, Bogotá, Colombia. Photo, by Hernán Díaz Giraldo.
13 Detail of Construction, Mesitas, South Barrow.
14 Main Statue, Mesita A, East Barrow. Height: 2.56 meters (8 feet, 4¾ inches).
15 Detail of Main Statue, Mesita A, East Barrow.
16 Guardian Statue, Mesita A, East Barrow. Height: 2 meters (6 feet, 6¾ inches).
17 Guardian Statue, Mesita A, West Barrow. Height: 1.74 meters (5 feet, 8½ inches).
18 Figure Holding Infant, Mesita B. Height: 1.15 meters (3 feet, 9¼ inches).
19 Alto de los Idolos.
20 Monolithic Sarcophagus at Alto de los Idolos. Length of coffin: 2.22 meters (7 feet, 3½ inches).

21 Stone Sarcophagus and Remains of Cist Grave at Alto de los Idolos. Length: 2.4 meters (7 feet, 10½ inches).

22 Monolithic Sarcophagus Surrounded by Slabs, Alto de los Idolos. Length: 2.4 meters (7 feet, 10½ inches).

23 Relief-carved Slab Covering Sarcophagus, Alto de los Idolos. Width of head: 84 centimeters (2 feet, 9 inches).

24 Columnar Statues from Mesita B, North Barrow. Average height: 1 meter (3 feet, 3¼ inches).

25 Columnar Statue from Mesita B, North Barrow. Height: 1 meter (3 feet, 3¼ inches).

26 Carved Head, La Estrella. Height: 75 centimeters (2 feet, 5½ inches).

27 Eroded Columnar Statue from Mesita B. Height: 80 centimeters (2 feet, 7½ inches).

28 Feline Columnar Statue from Mesita B. Height: 75 centimeters (2 feet, 5½ inches).

29 Two Guardian Figures, Mesita B, South Barrow. Heights: 1.45 meters (4 feet, 9 inches), 1.32 meters (4 feet, 4 inches).

30 Boulder Carving of Toad, Matanzas. Height: 88 centimeters (2 feet, 10½ inches); length: 2.33 meters (7 feet, 7¾ inches).

31 Carving of Jaguar and Woman, Ullumbe. Height: 89 centimeters (2 feet, 11 inches); length: 97 centimeters (3 feet, 2¼ inches).

32 Statue of Eagle Holding Snake, Mesita B. Height: 1.66 meters (5 feet, 5¼ inches).

33 Two Guardian Figures, Mesita A, East Barrow.

34 Statue with Marking on Chest, Mesita B. Height: 86 centimeters (2 feet, 9¾ inches).

35 Guardian Statue, Alto de las Piedras. Height: 1.84 meters (6 feet, ½ inch).

36 Detail of Guardian Statue, Alto de las Piedras.

37 Statue of Woman, Alto de las Piedras. Height: 1.4 meters (4 feet, 7 inches).

38 Female Statue with Feline Features. Height: 1.65 meters (5 feet, 5 inches).

39 Statue with Elaborate Headdress. Height: 1.54 meters (5 feet, ½ inch).

40 Feline Statue, Naranjo. Height: 89 centimeters (2 feet, 11 inches).

41 Statue with Conical Headdress. Height: 1.26 meters (4 feet, 1¼ inches) (see Plate 2).

42 Statue Holding Fish, Mesita B. Height: 1.3 meters (4 feet, 3¼ inches).

43 Female Statue with Cup. Height: 1.45 meters (4 feet, 9 inches).

44 Four-sided Relief Carving, Alto de los Idolos. Height: 1.95 meters (6 feet, 4¾ inches).

45 Statue of Crouching Woman, Naranjo. Height: 73 centimeters (2 feet, 4¾ inches).

46 Statue with Masklike Face, Quebradillas. Height: 1.68 meters (5 feet, 6¼ inches).

47 Statue with Masklike Face, Ullumbe. Height: 1.05 meters (3 feet, 5¼ inches).

48 Statue with Spiral-shaped Eyes, El Batán. Height: 1.24 meters (3 feet, 11¼ inches).

49 Figure with Hands on Shoulders, Alto de Lavaderos. Height: 87 centimeters (2 feet, 10¼ inches).

50 Statue with Bag, unknown provenance. Height: 1.28 meters (4 feet, 2½ inches).

51 Statue with Triangular Head, Mesita C. Height: 2.02 meters (6 feet, 7½ inches).

52 Statue with Triangular Headdress. Height: 1.75 meters (5 feet, 9 inches) (see Plate 2).

53 Statue with Flaring Skirt, El Cabuyal. Height: 1.13 meters (3 feet, 8½ inches).

54 Head of Seated Figure, Alto de Lavaderos. Height: 1.02 meters (3 feet, 4¼ inches).

55 Pot-bellied Jaguar, Mesita D. Height: 73 centimeters (2 feet, 4¾ inches).

56 Detail of Statue, Mesita B.

57 Statue with Squared Mouth, Mesita C. Height: 1.15 meters (3 feet, 9¼ inches). Collection Museo del Oro, Banco de la Republica, Bogotá, Colombia. Museum Photo.

58 Main Statue, West Barrow, Alto de los Idolos. Height: 1.6 meters (5 feet, 3 inches).

59 Statue with Head Trophy, Mesita B. Height: 1.77 meters (5 feet, 9¾ inches).

60 Detail of Statue with Head Trophy, Mesita B.

61 Guardian Statue, Mesita B. Height: 1.87 meters (6 feet, 1½ inches).

62 Guardian Statue, seen from left side, Mesita B.

63 Guardian Statue, Mesita B. Height: 1.85 meters (6 feet, ¾ inch).

64 Detail of Guardian Statue, Mesita B.

65 Statue Holding Snake, Mesita B. Height: 1.47 meters (4 feet, 10 inches).

66 Statue with Protruding Tongue, Ullumbe. Height: 82 centimeters (2 feet, 8¼ inches).

67 Statue with Two Staffs, Mesita C. Height: 1.82 meters (5 feet, 11¾ inches).

68 Thick Carved Slab, El Cabuyal. Height: 1.22 meters (4 feet).

69 Carved Slab, Alto de los Idolos. Visible height: 2.85 meters (9 feet, 4¼ inches).

70 Carved Slab, Mesita C. Height: 2.38 meters (7 feet, 9¾ inches).

71 Statue with "Double," Alto de Lavapatas. Height: 2.9 meters (9 feet, 6¼ inches).

72 Detail, Lower End of Secondary Figure, Alto de Lavapatas.

73 Detail of Side of Primary Figure's Head, Alto de Lavapatas.

74 Detail Showing Face of Primary Figure, Alto de Lavapatas.

75 Statue with "Double," Alto de las Piedras. Height: 3 meters (9 feet, 10 inches).

76 Detail Showing Face of Secondary Figure, Alto de las Piedras.

77 Double Statue Holding Child, Mesita B. Height: 4.25 meters (13 feet, 10½ inches).

78 Statue Holding Child, Mesita B. Height: 1.26 meters (4 feet, 1½ inches).

79 Statue with Nose Ornament, Mesita B. Height: 2.84 meters (9 feet, 3¾ inches).

80 Double-spouted Vessel of Isnos Period. Height: 10.8 centimeters (4¼ inches).

81 Anthropomorphic Vessel from Mesita B. Height: 17.5 centimeters (6¾ inches).

82 Double-spouted Vessel of Isnos Period. Height: 21 centimeters (4¼ inches).

83 Incised Bowl of Horqueta Period. Height: 9.2 centimeters (3½ inches).

84 Carved Head, Alto de Lavapatas. Height: 66 centimeters (2 feet, 2 inches).

85 Double-spouted Vessel of Isnos Period. Height: 9 centimeters (3½ inches).

86 Relief-carved Boulder, Ullumbe. Height: 1.46 meters (4 feet, 9½ inches).

87 Statue with Elongated Features, Alto de Lavaderos. Height: 1.46 meters (4 feet, 9½ inches).

88 Relief-carved Boulder, La Chaquira. Height: 2 meters (6 feet, 6¾ inches).

89 Relief-carved Boulders, La Chaquira.

90 Relief-carved Boulder, La Chaquira. Height: 2 meters (6 feet, 6¾ inches).

91 Bedrock Carving on Wall of Pool, Lavapatas.

92 Painted Bowl of Sombrerillos Period. Height: 5.2 centimeters (2 inches).

93 Statue with Staff, Quebradillas. Height: 1.75 meters (5 feet, 9 inches).

Figures

Index

Page numbers in italic refer to illustrations